Vera Lex

Journal of the International Natural Law Society

New Series Volume 7, Numbers 1&2   Winter 2006

COPYRIGHT © 2006
PACE UNIVERSITY PRESS
1 PACE PLAZA
NEW YORK, NY 10038

ISBN 0-944473-78-4
ISSN 0893-4851

CONTRIBUTORS
Address all submissions and correspondence to The Editor, VERA LEX, Pace University, Department of Philosophy & Religious Studies, 1 Pace Plaza, New York, NY 10038. Please send two copies of the paper submitted. Include adequate margins, double space everything (text, notes, works cited, quotations). Use U.S. spelling and punctuation style, (e.g. periods inside quotation marks; "double quotes" for opening and closing quotations). The University of Chicago Manual of Style, 13th Edition, is to be consulted regarding matters of style. Notes are to be numbered consecutively (in Arabic numerals) and placed at the bottom of the page.

SUBSCRIBERS
VERA LEX is published annually by Pace University Press, 41 Park Row, Room 1510, New York, NY 10038. Subscription price: $40. Please send all subscription inquiries to: PaceUP@services.pace.edu

INDEXING AND ABSTRACTING
VERA LEX is indexed in *Philosopher's Index.*
Copyright © 2006 by Pace University Press. Permission is required to reprint an article or part of an article.

VERA LEX, the journal of the International Natural Law Society, was established to communicate and dialogue on the subject of natural law and natural right, to introduce natural law philosophy into the mainstream of contemporary thought, and to strengthen the current revived interest in the discussion of morals and law and advance its historical research.

ROBERT CHAPMAN
Editor

VIRGINIA BLACK
Editor Emerita

Editorial Board

HAROLD BROWN
Department of Philosophy & Religious Studies, Pace University

MARK GOSSIAUX
Department of Philosophy, Loyola University, New Orleans

GREGORY J. KERR
Department of Philosophy & Theology, DeSales University

JOHN KRUMMEL
Department of Religion, Temple University

THOMAS O'SULLIVAN
Department of Philosophy & Religious Studies, Pace University

ALICE RAMOS
Department of Philosophy, St. John's University

LISA SIDERIS
Department of Religious Studies, Indiana University

PETER WIDULSKI
Loyola University School of Law, New Orleans

Why do we use a shell (*Nautilus pomplilus Linnaeus*) to symbolize *vera lex*? The logarithmic spiraling and overlapping chambers of the shell are endless. They suggest a patterned development and evolution that, by its radial and circular design, never comes to an end. This means that the shell is at once specific and real, while its form, like law, is abstract and ideal.

The pattern of a shell is, like good law, uniform, regular and reliable. It can therefore be anticipated and known. The pattern of a shell is balanced, like justice. *Una iustitia*.

A shell is a biological being. Like law, it has life and dynamic. It grows. (There is an average of thirty growth lines per chamber, one for every day in the lunar cycle, suggesting that a new chamber is put down each lunar month and a new growth line each day, thus recording two different natural rhythms, lunar and solar.)

The shell is a universal and common object known to everyone. A shell is not soft tissue easily destroyed. And yet, like liberty, it is fragile in certain respects if stepped on with an iron boot. It has to be guarded with vigilance or it is crushed.

In every shell lives a nautilus. If the shell is law, the nautilus (snail) is a person—it is alive—person and law. Their destinies, like person and law, are interdependent.

Vera Lex

leges innumerae, una iustitia

CONTENTS

NEW SERIES VOLUME 7, NUMBERS 1 & 2   WINTER 2006

GUEST EDITORIAL   John W.M. Krummel   1

FEATURED ARTICLES: NATURAL LAW THEORY & ASIAN THOUGHT

The Problem of the Unjust Law in   R. Joseph Harte   7
Western and East Asian Legal
Philosophy: The Case of Korea

The Neo-Confucian Theory of *Li*,   Peter P. Cvek   37
the Goodness of Human Nature,
and the Natural Law

Early Buddhist Inclusion of   Victor Forte   59
Intentionality in the Laws of Causation

FEATURE

The Third Wave? The Generation   Eric Engle   77
Theory of Human Rights

BOOK REVIEWS

Charles Taylor, *Multiculturalism and*   Charles Brian   127
"The Politics Of Recognition"   McAdams

Howard Kainz, *Natural Law:*   Robert Chapman   131
An Introduction and Re-Examination

ANNOTATED BIBLIOGRAPHY   John W.M. Krummel   135

CONTRIBUTORS   161

GUEST EDITORIAL

The theme of this issue of *Vera Lex* is dedicated to the relationship between natural law theory and Asian philosophy and religion. At first one may wonder how the two may even be brought into dialogue. The historical origins of natural law theory are usually traced to the medieval Scholastic (hence, Christian, specifically Roman Catholic) and Aristotelian philosophical schools of the West. What would thought-systems originating in "the East" have to offer to a natural law theorist coming from the Christian—or even post-Christian secular—"West"? On top of this one may even question whether there is any "philosophy" outside of the Greco-European tradition from which we have inherited the very term "philosophy" (*philosophia*). Although I cannot hope to answer adequately that latter question here in this short introduction, suffice it to say that the search for wisdom (*sophia*), the pursuit of truth, is a universal human endeavor, over which Western Europeans can claim no special privilege at the expense of others. Highly systematic and developed modes of speculation and thought in general have evolved in different parts of the world outside of the traditions that have inherited Greek concepts (that is, beyond the Western European, Islamic, and Russian traditions of thought). And I believe they have much to offer to the European or Western philosopher, in terms of content (ideas) as well as of methods or modes of thinking. Nor can we afford to confine or isolate ourselves within what we regard as our "own tradition," when the world is, and has been, rapidly changing shape due to its so-called "globalization," bringing together previously separated cultural horizons, whether it be through peaceful integration or through violent conflict. As philosophers, we can no longer just ignore, or pretend the non-existence of, those speculative traditions of the extra-Greco-European world. Especially today when the collapsing of cultural worlds can lead to violent outbreak, it is necessary to engage in dialogue, to exchange ideas, and to be willing to learn from—or at least learn *about*—one another's insights. This is so, especially if one is not to fall into the trap of reducing one's *other* to one's *own* pre-conceptions and stereotypical images of the other. Hence we need to be weary of hypostatizing "West" and "East" as monolithic entities closed off from each other—a point that I shall discuss further below. The situation calls for an openness to the very possibility that the wisdom or truth we seek may not be in the sole possession of "the West"—especially if our philosophizing is to be relevant to the "globalized" world of today. It is in light of this contemporary situation that I hope the discussions of "natural law" *vis-à-vis* Asian philosophy—even as the very concept and theory of "natural law" hails its origin from Greco-European philosophy—in this issue of *Vera Lex* will make a contribution to the exchange of ideas in the contemporary world.

The various versions of natural law theory that emerged in the West postulate, in different ways, a moral law "higher" than those limited by the contingencies of human invention. Their proponents have claimed certain laws to be universally valid, hence "natural" as fundamental principles with theological and/or rational grounding. They have defined ethics, on the basis of the natural law, to be one that can be discovered by the rational analysis of human nature and often in its relation to the cosmos or the divine law-maker. This implies a connection between prescriptive rules and descriptive principles, between the normative and the explanatory, between the ethical and the metaphysical (cosmological or ontological) or epistemological, between the "ought" of human behavior and the "is" in the order of reality or of rationality. Philosophizing with the above-mentioned global context in mind, this leads to the question of whether there are any notions outside of the Western tradition comparable to the natural law idea of the West. And if so, how similar are they? How do they contrast? For example, the Indian concept of *dharma* in both the Hindu and Buddhist contexts has social, ethical, and cosmic, normative and explanatory senses, especially in connection with the notion of *karma*. And in the Chinese traditions, the notions of *li* (in the sense of ritual, ceremony, propriety, custom, etc.), *li* (in the sense of patterning, principle)—those two senses of *li* are homonyms with distinct meanings as I shall explain below—, and *tao* (way), together with the related ideas of *jen* (humanity), *t'ien* (heaven), or *t'ai-chi* (great ultimate), each have both normative and descriptive connotations, entailing both human and cosmic dimensions. How different or similar are these ideas and doctrines in relation to Western natural law theories? Can the normativity they provide for human behavior likewise be said to be "natural" (in the sense of natural law theory)?

The three feature articles of this issue on "Natural Law and Asian Philosophy" cover the traditions of Buddhism and Confucianism, or more specifically early Indian Buddhism, Confucianism, Legalism, and Neo-Confucianism. In the opening piece, "The Problem of the Unjust Law in Western and East Asian Legal Philosophy: The Case of Korea," R. Joseph Harte compares East Asian (Chinese and Korean) Confucian thought and Western natural law theory and their respective responses to the question of "unjust law." In doing so he covers their respective debates concerning the role of law in society against the Legalists (for the Confucians) and against the proponents of positive law (for natural law theory). He shows how natural law theory and Confucian thought, while both providing alternatives to unjust law, do so from distinct premises in their views concerning "nature" or the "natural" in relation to man and society. The next article, "The Neo-Confucian Theory of *Li*, the Goodness of Human Nature, and the Natural Law" by Peter P. Cvek, takes a look at the connection between the Confucian-Mencian doctrine of the goodness of human nature and the Sung Neo-Confucian metaphysical concept of *li*. Cvek compares and contrasts the role *li* is taken to play in founding the goodness of human nature with the role played by the idea of natural law in the West, especially in Thomism. For readers who may not be familiar with the Chinese traditions of thought, I should point out here that while both Harte and Cvek refer to *li*, they are not speaking of the same thing. Rather they are homonyms. As briefly alluded to above, these are distinct concepts with different meanings, represented by two different ideographs but both pronounced "*li*." The *li* that Harte refers to means "ritual" or "rite," and signifies the code of appropriate interpersonal conduct or behavior. This concept is of central significance for the earlier form of Confucianism that began with Confucius (551-479 BCE) and became the state orthodoxy during the Han Dynasty (202 BCE – 220 CE). The *li* that is the central topic of Cvek's paper on the other hand, is of a different ideographic character and means "principle" but also more literally "pattern" or "order." This concept is of central significance for the much later intellectual movement that Western scholars have come to call "Neo-Confucianism," and in particular the school called *li-hsüeh* or the "study/school of *li*," established and popularized during the Sung Dynasty (960-1279 CE). Despite being homonyms with different senses, both concepts however provide possible junctures for discussing the idea of the natural law vis-à-vis Chinese thought, Confucian and Neo-Confucian. For example, *li* as "ritual" or "rite" in classical Confucianism has the sense of rules for appropriate behavior in interpersonal relations. To model one's inter-personal behavior and relations with others in accordance with it would allegedly allow one to realize one's human *nature*, i.e., to become a *humane* person or a man of *jen* (the virtue of humaneness or compassion). And the *li* studied by Neo-Confucianism that is the underlying "patterning" of the universe, serving as "principles" that structure the flow of *ch'i* ("material energy") to constitute the cosmos of many things, also has moral implications, relating to the ethical norms that structure human activity. Both concepts of *li* may provide windows for viewing the "natural law" of the Western tradition in a new light.

The same can be said for the Indian concepts of *karma* and *dharma*. *Karma* literally means "action" but has come to designate for the Indian religious mind the cosmic law of "action-and-reaction" or "cause-and-effect" that anything one thinks, says, or does, has its moral consequences, or in popular parlance, "what comes around goes around." And *dharma*, which has different significances in different contexts, in general means something like the "order" that holds everything together. In the traditional Hindu social context, *dharma* means one's social duties and obligations. In Buddhism it has different connotations. First it means the "truth" that Gautama the Buddha experienced in regard to the universe while meditating, and secondly it comes to mean the "doctrines" taught by the Buddha about the truth. If Buddhism seeks to provide a path for overcoming the *karmic* nature of reality that fuels the *samsaric* (i.e., reincarnation) cycle of the physical world that traps us in a perpetual rat-race, then the *dharma* it preaches must have something to do with that *karmic* nature of reality. In any case both notions about the cosmos and reality in general seem to have ethical implications. To what extent then is the Buddhist understanding of moral law, viewed in light of these concepts, comparable to Western natural law theory? The last and final feature article, "Early Buddhist Inclusion of Intentionality in the Laws of Causation" by Victor Forte tackles some of these questions while focusing upon the relationships between *karma*, mental intention and physical action. How does the *karmic* law of cause-and-effect or action-and-reaction work? What gives rise to *karmic* consequences? Is it our intentions, or even mental states *per se*, or our physical actions, that give rise to *karma*? Can we look to intentions alone as the cause of *karma* or is it really the physical actions that are morally significant in the *karmic* process? In light of such *karmic* causality, what moral implications may we obtain from the "natural law" of the *dharma*?

What we have here then are three papers on East Asian and Indian, Confucian and Buddhist, thinking, that may open some new windows for viewing the natural law and its various interpretations in a new light shining from "the East." However in mentioning "the East" here, we should be weary of hypostatizing such geographical-cultural regions—as in "East" vs. "West"—as monolithic and unalterable absolutes. Lumping Indian thought together with East Asian thought as one "tradition" is certainly problematic, and one could argue that Indian traditions are just as distinct from the East Asian traditions as they are from the Western philosophical tradition. The boundaries of "East" and "West" are each fluid and encompass a variety of traditions within. It is this fluidity and multiplicity, as opposed to being closed monoliths, that allow for genuine cross-cultural dialogue amidst difference/s—as opposed to any proselytizing imposition of alleged "universals" on one's part upon *others*. New and meaningful philosophical insights that may be of relevance for today's world, including insights in regard to the natural law, should then emerge.

To complement the three feature articles on Asian thought, we have added a fourth paper to this issue. This final paper, "The Third Wave? The Generation Theory of Human Rights" by Eric Engle, discusses the concept of human rights within the global context and in relation to theories of natural law, its universality and its evolution. Its look to the concept of rights from an international or global angle should be of interest to readers of this issue of *Vera Lex* dedicated to the connection of natural law theory and Asian thought.[1]

---

[1] I do however want to point out to the readers that the author's claim that Taoism is 'idealist' (p. 101) is controversial and can be disputed.

FEATURED ARTICLES

THE PROBLEM OF THE UNJUST LAW IN WESTERN AND EAST ASIAN LEGAL PHILOSOPHY: THE CASE OF KOREA
R. Joseph Harte

INTRODUCTION

The problem of the unjust law, containing at its core some of the most fundamental questions of law and morality, is as ancient as the study of law and philosophy itself. The Greeks first took up the question over twenty-four hundred years ago when they asked whether "the right and the just" is so by nature or whether it is so by custom and enactment.[1] Since that time, the question has had, according to Pound, "a long and fruitful history in philosophical jurisprudence."[2] Of course, given the inevitable tailspins into which the question sends even the most accomplished thinkers, one may wonder whether the history of the question has indeed been fruitful. In fact, the problem to this day presents a recurring impasse between Natural Law proponents and strict legal positivists. Nonetheless, regardless of where one stands on the fruitfulness of the question, one can at least agree that its history has indeed been long.

Looking beyond the shores of Western legal philosophy, one might also agree that the question has traveled far and wide. The question of whether a law is just has a rich (and just as ancient) history in the political, social and legal philosophies of East Asia. The Confucians and the Chinese Legalists long ago wrangled over the place of law in society and its attendant moral value and function.[3] The almost antithetical positions staked out by these two ancient schools of thought continue to have an

---

[1] Roscoe Pound, *An Introduction to the Philosophy of Law* (New Haven: Yale University Press, 1954), p. 7 [hereinafter *Philosophy of Law*]; *See also* Huntington Cairns, *Legal Philosophy from Plato to Hegel* (Baltimore: Johns Hopkins Press, 1949), p. 25.

[2] Pound, *Philosophy of Law*, *supra*, p. 7.

[3] *See generally* R. P. Peerenboom, *Law and Morality in Ancient China: The Silk Manuscripts of Huang-Lao* (Albany: State University of New York Press, 1993); David L. Hall & Roger T. Ames, *Thinking Through Confucius* (Albany: State University of New York Press, 1987); Fung Yu-Lan, *A History of Chinese Philosophy*, Vol. I (Princeton: Princeton University Press, 1952), pp. 312-14 [hereinafter *Chinese Philosophy*].

impact on contemporary attitudes in East Asia toward the role of law in society, its meaning for social and moral order, and the reception of Western legal concepts.[4]

Nowhere is this more true than in the history of modern legal development in Korea. In his various works on the subject, Pyong Choon Hahm characterized the Korean legal system as one that is in many ways '*alegalistic*' when compared to a *legalistic* Western tradition.[5] Because Korean government and society for nearly 500 years founded itself upon Neo-Confucian principles,[6] which posit that a need for 'laws' represents a failure of human order, instead opting for a social order founded on *interpersonal relationship*, Hahm argues that Korean society is one that finds a reliance on law and legal proceedings not only alien but frightful.[7] In Hahm's view, this is because the Confucian basis of the Korean social order sees law as merely a tool of the ruler.[8] For a humane society, strict legal principles are not the answer. Rather, only the moral principles of interpersonal relationship can result in a truly just society.

However, while it may be true that the Confucian worldview rejects the notion of law as the fundamental principle of a humane social order, a simple review of the Korean historical record reveals that Korea has had a long history of extensively developed legal codes full of the kind of prohibitions and punishments that are common to all legal codes. Application

---

[4] *See, e.g.,* Kang, Jung In, "The Rule of Law and the Rule of Virtue: On the Necessity for Their Mutual Integration," *Korea Journal*, vol. 43, no. 1 (Spring 2003), p. 233.

[5] Hahm, Pyong Choon, "The Korean Political Tradition and Law," in Hahm, Pyong Choon, *The Korean Political Tradition and Law: Essays in Korean Law and Legal History* (Seoul: Hollym Corp., 1967), p. 6 [hereinafter *Korean Political Tradition*]; Hahm, Pyong Choon, "The Traditional Patterns of Authoritative Symbols and the Judicial Process in Korea," in Hahm, Pyong Choon, *Korean Jurisprudence, Politics and Culture* (Seoul: Yonsei University Press, 1986), p. 7 [hereinafter *Korean Jurisprudence*].

[6] Confucianism reached Korea through the writings of the Chinese Neo-Confucian, Chu Hsi (1130-1200 A.D.), and his predecessors of the Sung period of China (late 12th century). These teachings became the established doctrine of officialdom under the Korean Yi Dynasty (1392-1910). *See* Hahm, *Korean Political Tradition, supra* note 5, pp. 8-9; *see also* Martina Deuchler, *The Confucian Transformation of Korea: A Study of Society and Ideology* (Cambridge, MA: Harvard University Press, 1992); Wm. Theodore de Bary and JaHyun Haboush eds., *The Rise of Neo-Confucianism in Korea* (New York: Columbia University Press, 1985).

[7] Hahm, *Korean Political Tradition, supra* note 5, pp. 19-21.

[8] *Id.*

of the word '*alegal*' to Korean legal thought is therefore somewhat problematic.9 Clearly, the history of laws in a Confucian based society such as Korea indicates a use of positivistic legal rules and conventions aimed at ordering society at least in terms of the most basic variables of crime and punishment. But the overarching antithetical approach to the concept of law as having anything to do with ultimate humanity suggests the existence of a significant gap between concepts of law and concepts of morality in East Asian jurisprudence.

It has been suggested that this gap parallels the Natural Law/Positive Law debate in Western jurisprudence.10 However, while similarities between the Chinese Legalists and Western Positivists may be compelling, a close analysis of the Confucian worldview and that of Natural Law proponents in the West, at least on the question of 'unjust law,' reveals important differences between natural law thinking and Confucian concepts of law. Viewing this distinction in the context of unjust law offers a convenient focal point for a comparative analysis of the Natural Law/Positive Law debate in Western jurisprudence and the Confucian/Legalist debate in East Asian legal philosophy. This is because the problem of the unjust law is often the point at which Western conceptions of natural law and positive law part ways.11 Exploring a sim-

---

9 To be sure, Dr. Hahm seems to take note of this problem in a later writing when he states: "Inasmuch as the culture to be studied [i.e. Korean culture] is so different from the West as to be characterized as 'alegal,' the conventional Anglo-American concept of law itself will be of little use for our purpose. A conclusion that traditional Korea had no 'law' would serve no constructive purpose." Hahm, *Korean Jurisprudence, supra* note 5, p. 7. By his use of the term 'alegal,' then, at least in this second writing, it is clear that Hahm is not speaking of the existence or absence of laws, but rather of a particular *orientation* toward law itself. Unfortunately, the use of the term in both writings creates a sense of fundamental antithesis between the Korean and Western legal traditions that is perhaps unnecessarily dualistic in nature.

10 *See, e.g.*, Joseph Needham, *Science and Civilization in China*, Vol. 2 (Cambridge, England: University Press, 1954), p. 519 (associating the Western notion of natural law (*jus naturale*) with the Chinese concept of ritual action *li*, and positive law with the Chinese notion of law as punishment (*fa*)).

11 *See* Peerenboom, *supra* note 3, p. 118 ("In coming to terms with this enigmatic concept, we found it helpful to contrast natural law with legal positivism, key differentia being that the latter does not require law to display any necessary relation to morality to be valid. This was referred to as the minimum separation thesis. Natural law proponents deny the minimum separation thesis, asserting that '"an unjust law is no law at all."').

ilar distinction between law and morality in the East Asian context not only sheds light on the handling of the problem in the East Asian tradition but also serves to place in relief some of the basic assumptions underlying Western conceptions of natural law and the relationship between law and morality.[12]

With these considerations in mind, my goal in this study is to compare the responses of both Western jurisprudence and East Asian legal philosophy to the problem of the unjust law. I argue that despite the apparent similarities between concepts of natural law and Confucian legal philosophy, the Western and East Asian legal traditions have in fact responded to the eventuality of unjust law in very different ways. This difference can be explained by a critical divergence in the foundational principles that inform the normative views of the two traditions. Briefly, while Western Natural Law proponents in discussions on law and morality often begin with notions of 'pre-social man,' or *man-in-nature*, who then leaves nature to become *man-in-society*, Confucian thought is founded upon notions of *man-in-society as an expression of nature*. This distinction leads to very different views regarding the role of law in society and the problem of dealing with the advent of unjust law.

I develop this argument by looking to examples of traditional East Asian legal philosophy and its specific manifestations in Korean legal history. This is followed by a comparative analysis of some of the basic notions underpinning Western concepts of natural law and Confucian legal philosophy. The ideas developed there are then applied to the prob-

---

[12] On the relationship between comparative law and jurisprudence, see Catherine Dauvergne, "New Directions for Jurisprudence," in Catherine Dauvergne (ed.), *Jurisprudence for an Interconnected Globe* (Aldershot, Hampshire, England; Burlington, VT: Ashgate, 2003); William Twining, "The Province of Jurisprudence Re-examined," in Catherine Dauvergne ed., *Jurisprudence for an Interconnected Globe* (Aldershot, Hampshire, England; Burlington,VT: Ashgate, 2003). Andrew Harding & Esin Örücü eds., *Comparative Law in the 21st Century* (London; New York: Kluwer Academic, 2002); William L. Twining, *Globalisation and Legal Theory* (London: Butterworths, 2000); Alan Watson, *Legal Transplants: An Approach to Comparative Law* (Charlottesville: University Press of Virginia, 1974), pp.6-8; For a fully realized development of the notion of a 'comparative jurisprudence' as an independent discipline in its own right, see William Ewald, "Comparative Jurisprudence (I): What was it like to try a rat?," *University of Pennsylvania Law Review*, vol. 143 (June, 1995), p. 1889; William Ewald, "Comparative Jurisprudence (II): The Logic of Legal Transplants," *American Journal of Comparative Law*, vol. 43 (Fall, 1995), p. 489.

lem of the unjust law in general, as a matter of comparative jurisprudence. Accordingly, Parts I and II review the legal philosophies of the Chinese Legalists and the Confucians respectively. Part III presents an historical survey of the way in which these two schools of thought may have competed for supremacy in Yi Dynasty Korea. I posit that the tension between the two doctrines may have had the unexpected result of achieving a balance of power between officialdom and monarchy. Part IV goes on to examine the foundational divergence between Western notions of natural law and Confucian thought as it pertains to questions of law and morality. Finally, Part V draws on this foundational divergence to explain the differing approaches to the problem of unjust law in Western and East Asian thinking.

I THE CHINESE LEGALISTS

Chinese Legalist doctrines began to flourish as a response to the disintegration of feudalism in China during the 7th-3rd century B.C.[13] Prior to this disintegration, feudalism had allowed for a system of social order that was largely maintained on the basis of face-to-face relationships. States, limited in size, were subdivided into houses, and the heads of these houses governed those below by a system of social propriety focused on the proper functioning of interpersonal relationship. The rules supporting this system were known as "*li*."[14] This code of conduct also guided the interactions between and among the nobles themselves.[15] With the disintegration of the feudal order, the continuation of such a personalized system of social propriety became practically untenable.[16] The break down of the feudal system also allowed for the ascension of a powerful monarchy in its place. As the noble class declined, the State, as represented in the person of the monarch, with its attendant bureaucracy, became increasingly more powerful. In addition, the common people

---

[13] Fung, *Chinese Philosophy*, *supra* note 3, p. 312. For an interesting parallel between the Chinese context and the underlying socio-political forces that may have given rise to questions of law and justice in the Greek world, see Pound, *Philosophy of Law*, *supra* note 1, pp. 4-6.

[14] Fung, *Chinese Philosophy*, *supra* note 3, p. 312.

[15] *Id.*, p. 313.

[16] *See id.*

gained greater and greater freedom from the heads of the great houses.[17] As a result of these changes, the problem of social order became a far more complex undertaking.

In response, various states began to promulgate explicit codes of law.[18] For example, in 543 B.C., the state of Cheng composed its first criminal code, and in 513 B.C., the state of Chin is said to have "inscribed penal laws . . . upon bronze tripods which it had cast."[19] Hence, "[t]he great political tendency of the time was a movement from feudal rule to a government by rulers possessing absolute power; from government by customary morality (*li*), and by individuals, to government by law."[20]

It was the Legalists who supplied the theoretical arguments in defense of this new emphasis on 'government by law.'[21] The doctrines developed by the Legalists are traditionally divided into three schools. The first group, headed by *Shen Tao*, proclaimed the essential importance of 'power' or 'authority' (*shih*).[22] The second group, led by *Shang Yang* (died 338 B.C.), emphasized the role and purposes of law (*fa*) in itself,[23] while the third school, led by *Shen Pu-Hai* (died 337 B.C.), emphasized the importance of 'methods of government' or 'statecraft' (*shu*).[24] These three schools were later brought together into a unified system of thought by *Han Fei* (died 233 B.C.), who held that all three factors were essential to a social order regulated by the instruments of law.[25]

Regarding the relationship between power (*shih*) and social order, *Han Fei* explains in the *Kuantzu* (ch. 67):

> [I]f there is an intelligent ruler above, who is the possessor of authority (*shih*) whereby he can rule with absolute certainty, his multitudes of subjects will not dare to do wrong. The rea-

---

[17] *Id.*
[18] *Id.*
[19] *Id.*
[20] *Id.*, p. 312.
[21] *Id.*, p. 316.
[22] *Id.*, p. 318.
[23] *Id.*
[24] *Id.*, pp. 318-319.
[25] *Id.*, p. 320.

> son why these multitudes of subjects do not dare to deceive their ruler is not because they love him, but because they fear his awe inspiring power (*shih*) . . . because they fear his laws and commands. He rests in an authority (*shih*) requiring obligatory respect, so as to keep in order the subjects who must obey him.[26]

The passage ends with a direct admonition of the kind of power that is based on interpersonal factors: "That the ruler is honored and his subjects are meek, does not come through attempts to cousin them. It is through the supremacy of the (ruler's) power."[27] Thus, according to the Legalists, social order is to be squarely founded upon the fear of a ruler wielding absolute power.

Wielding such power, the ruler uses law (*fa*) for the sole purpose of maintaining social order by means of reward and punishment. The school led by *Shang Yang* elaborated on the specific role and nature of laws utilized in this manner:

> Laws are the models for the empire and the representative standards for all affairs . . . the intelligent ruler carries out punishments according to the law . . . so when the officials have law for what they enforce, the people obey them, and when they lack law, the people stop (obeying them) . . .[28]

> Laws serve to provide the models for the orders promulgated by the officials; that penalties will be kept fresh in the minds of the people; that rewards will go to those who are observant of the laws; and that punishment will go to those who violate orders.[29]

Under this view, then, laws are a list of rules and standards that provide the justification for penalties. Guaranteeing proper observance of the

---

[26] *Id.*, p. 318.
[27] *Id.*, p. 318-319.
[28] *Id.*, p. 321 (quoting from the *Kuan-tzu*, ch. 67, *chuan* 21).
[29] *Id.*, p. 319 (quoting from the *HanFeitzu*, ch. 43, *chuan* 17).

law rests upon the threat of punishment or the promise of reward. Law has, therefore, a purely *punitive* function and the ruler makes use of this punitive nature of law to maintain absolute power:

> [T]he intelligent ruler leads and governs his subjects . . . by means of two handles. These two handles are penalty and benevolence . . . when the ruler uses penalty and benevolence, his multitude of subjects stand in fear of his majesty.[30]

In other words, law is the instrument of power:

> All ruling of the empire must be done by utilizing . . . rewards and punishments. . . . When rewards and punishments may be employed, interdicts and commands may be established, and the way of government is completed. The ruler holds on to these handles so as to rest in his power (*shih*), and hence his orders operate and his interdicts serve to prevent.[31]

Thus, the role of Law, having a purely punitive function, is to serve as the singular means by which the masses are subjected to the absolute power of the ruler.

'Methods' or 'statecraft' (*shu*) represents the means by which the ruler is to use the punitive nature of law to gain power. The works of Shen Pu-Hai have been lost. However, his works are mentioned in the *Han-Feitzu* regarding the indispensability of law (*fa*) and methods (*shu*) to the maintenance of absolute power (*shih*) by the ruler:

> If the ruler does not have his methods (*shu*), there will be weakness above. If his ministers do not have their laws (*fa*), there will be confusion below. Neither of these can be dispensed with. They are both the instruments of emperors and kings.[32]

In sum, absolute power, laws, and the methods by which law is used

---

[30] *Id.*, p. 326 (quoting from the *Han-Feitzu*, ch. 7, *chuan* 2).

[31] *Id.* (quoting from the *Han-Feitzu*, ch. 48, *chuan* 18).

[32] *Id.*, p. 319 (quoting from the *Han-Feitzu*, ch. 43, *chuan* 17).

to maintain power, are mutually dependent in the Chinese Legalist view of law and its moral function in society. This association of absolute power with law and statecraft represents the fundamental quality of the Legalist school. In fact, if we look at the philosophy in terms of the goal it proclaims and the means by which that goal is to be achieved, we can see that the relationship between absolute power and law is more than a simple association borne out by logic. Instead, absolute power is the ultimate goal of the Legalist ruler, while law itself represents the means by which that power is achieved and maintained. This perhaps explains the purely punitive nature ascribed to law in East Asian legal philosophy. For what else but a punitive kind of Law could be utilized to maintain absolute power?

II THE CONFUCIAN VIEW OF LAW

The emphasis by the Chinese Legalists on utilization of punitive law as a means to absolute power provides the basis for Confucianism's complete rejection of law as the foundation of a humane social order. This rejection is both political and philosophical in its roots. As noted earlier, the political tendency of the Warring States period in China was toward an absolute monarchy at the expense of an aristocratic class that held its power in a feudalistic social order. Maintaining its power over a social order legitimized by an idealized set of interpersonal codes, this group would have felt threatened by the notion of an absolute ruler wielding punitive laws over all and anyone below. According to the *Tso Chuan*, Confucius had the following to say about the tendencies toward Legalism in the state of Chin:[33]

> Chin is going to ruin! It has lost its proper rules. Chin ought to keep the laws and rules which T'ang Shu received for the regulation of his people, and the ministers and great officers ought to keep them in their several positions. Then the people would be able to honor the upper classes, and the upper classes would be able to preserve their inheritances. There would be nothing wrong with the noble or the mean. We should have what might

---

[33] The reader will recall that it was the state of Chin that had erected bronze tripods inscribed with penal laws. *See* n. 19, *supra*.

be called the proper rule . . . But now when those rules are abandoned, and tripods with the penal laws on them are cast instead, the people will study the tripods. How will they then honor their men of rank, and what will the nobles do? When there is no distinction of noble and mean, how can a state continue to exist?[34]

Here, Legalism is condemned as a direct threat not only to the ideology that supported the position of the noble class, but to the very existence of the State itself.

Of course, to Western ears, the Confucian emphasis on the preservation of the upper classes may sound alarming given the Western movement toward liberal democracy in modern times. However, it is important to keep in mind two points on this matter. First, what the Confucians were rejecting was the wielding of absolute power by a single ruler. They reject this absolute power through appeal to what is viewed as the moral order of the time. While this moral order is not founded upon a Divine source, as in the classic exposition of Natural Law in the West, but rather by reference to the interpersonal relationships of society, it nonetheless represents an appeal to a higher order of moral strictures in contradistinction to a notion of law that is purely punitive in nature. Second, it is important to remember that it was also the noble classes in the West who sought to appeal to a 'higher morality' in their efforts at reigning in the absolute power of the monarch. The only difference between the Confucians in the East and the Natural Law proponents in the West on this point is that the former appealed to the morality of a social order that supported their status, while the latter appealed to a morality of Divine origin. Furthermore, lest the reader should think this latter appeal was taken out of a purely selfless reference to faith, it may be worth noting that in a system whereby the absolute power of the monarch was derived from the Divine, it was perhaps no accident that the justification for the restraint on that power should also come from the Divine. In a similar fashion, at least on a pure-

---

[34] Fung, *Chinese Philosophy*, *supra* note 3, p. 314 (quoting from the *Tso Chuan*, p. 732). Note that when Confucius calls for Chin to "keep the laws and rules which T'ang Shu received," he presents those "laws and rules" in contrast to the "*penal* laws" of the tripods.

ly functional level, Confucian learning, itself a staple of the Chinese noble class, provided the intellectual justification for its rejection of absolute rule by punitive law.

In opposition to a political system founded entirely upon law, then, Confucianism argued for a social order regulated by the principles of *li*. For maintaining order in society, these principles are described as having two primary functions. The first is the control of human emotions to prevent public disorder: "The *li*, following human feelings, act as regulators and refiners of them, so as to keep the people within bounds."[35] The second function is to provide a system of rules by which the various relationships of society are defined and maintained:

> Without [*li*] . . . there would be no means of distinguishing the positions of ruler and subject, superior and inferior, old and young; and no means of keeping separate the relations between man and woman, father and son, elder and younger brother, and of conducting the intercourse between contracting families in a marriage, and the frequency (of the reciprocities between friends) or their infrequency.[36]

According to the Confucian ethic, paying proper attention to these relationships not only avoids social confusion but also provides the ultimate basis for moral guidance:

> The *li* are that whereby are determined (the observances toward) close and far relatives, points which may cause suspicion or doubt are settled, similarity and difference are differentiated, and *right and wrong are made clear.*[37]

The *li*, therefore, serve to define and regulate a moral order that is dependent both upon clearly delineated social relationships and the proper observance of conduct that is appropriate to the interaction between the individuals within those relationships. With this in mind, it easy to see how such a system would provide ample soil for the explanation of social conflict, and the concurrent sense of injustice that is the companion of all

---

[35] *Id.*, p. 338 (quoting the *Li Chi*, chap. XXVII).
[36] *Id.*, p. 339 (quoting the *Li Chi*, chap. XXIV).
[37] *Id.*, p. 339 (quoting from the *Li Chi*, chap. I)(emphasis added).

conflict, by referring to the failure of the involved parties to pay proper attention to their social relationship. Also, since relationship *defines* the social system itself, a break down in the attention paid to relationships represents a breakdown in the social order as a whole.[38] Furthermore, since a concept of social order that is based on proper attention to interpersonal relationship is in itself, according to the Confucian view, the very definition of 'humanity,' breakdown in the social order becomes a breakdown in humanity. Coming full circle, then, we can see why a system that does not take into account the value of social relationship, but rather resorts to the use of laws for the foundation of its social order, would be perceived as 'inhuman' since ignorance of social relationship ignores social order, and thereby ignores humanity.

This also explains why the Confucians would see Chinese Legalism as a threat to the very existence of the State itself. Under the Confucian view, Legalism ignored that which *defines* Society. Absence of attention to this defining quality could only result in an absence of Society itself. Chinese Legalism is therefore taken to be a philosophy that is diametrically opposed to a system of social order based on *li* because it proclaims the use of absolute power, supported by impersonal law, rather than the supremacy of the proper observance of social relationships as a guiding principle for human social order. In one of the few instances where the term sometimes translated as "justice" (*i*) appears in the ancient texts, it appears as a companion of *li*, juxtaposed to notions of law and punishment. Placing the principles of *li* and justice on one side of the ledger, and laws and commands on the other, fundamentally different results for the social order are expected:

> When there is government through *li* and standards of justice (*i*), *li* and justice are accumulated; when it is by punishments and penalties, there is an accumulation of these. When these last are accumulated, the people feel resentment and revolt. When *li* and standards of justice are accumulated, the people are in a state of harmony and feel affection. Thus, rulers of all periods have been alike in desiring that the people be good, but

---

[38] By this I mean to say that the social system is not *created by* a delineation of social positions, but rather, the social system *is* a delineation of social position. That is to say, a proponent of this position would ask the rhetorical question, "What is social *order* if not social *position*?"

> the methods they have used to bring about such goodness have differed. Some have led them with virtuous teachings, while others have driven them by laws and commands. When they are led by virtuous teachings, these virtuous teachings are practiced and the people are peaceful and contented. When they are driven by laws and commands, the laws and commands go to extremes and the people are sad and pitiful. The feelings of sadness or contentment are responsible respectively for calamity or blessing. [39]

The lines between the principles of *li* and a system of laws based on punishment and reward are clearly marked. According to the Confucians, some societies are led by "virtuous teachings," while others are led by "laws and commands." The former has the result of creating a "peaceful and contented" society, while the latter will have the result of "sadness and calamity," perhaps even culminating in outright revolt. The dichotomy in Confucian thinking between morality and justice on the one hand, and law on the other, could not be more clear.

For purposes of the present of study, what is essential to note in the language cited above is that even in the Confucian response to Chinese Legalism, laws continue to be viewed as a means of control through reward and punishment. That is, the punitive nature of law is taken by both the Legalists and the Confucians to be the *only* nature of law. Furthermore, laws are clearly differentiated from a concept of justice. Standards of justice (*i*) are associated with a positive social order while 'laws and commands' are associated with one that is ultimately disastrous. Hence, in both the Confucian and Chinese Legalist view of what is the most effective and proper means for achieving social order, laws serve a purely punitive function. The only difference is that one accepts the 'legalistic' approach to social order, while the other rejects it entirely.

It is perhaps this pervasive characterization of law as nothing more than a set of rules serving only the punitive, and therefore having in itself no reference to 'justice,' that leads to the confusion between the traditional Korean sense of legality and what law has come to mean in the West. As Hahm points out,

---

[39] Fung, *Chinese Philosophy*, *supra* note 3, p. 341 (quoting from the *Li Chi* of the Elder Tai, *chuan* 2).

> In European languages, the word that is used for law is also used for denoting . . . justice. Justice without law is inconceivable in those countries. Indeed the purpose of law is to realize justice . . . . In the Korean tradition, law has never been synonymous with justice.[40]

While the role of law has in fact come to mean something broader than mere punishment in the Western tradition, the Korean tradition associates law with, *and only with*, punishment and control. It is perhaps for this reason that the Western penchant for laws is instinctively rejected by Korean social values as something less than humane.

III CONFUCIANISM AND CHINESE LEGALISM IN YI DYNASTY KOREA: OFFICIALDOM VS. MONARCHY

> As for the laws, let them be recorded on the registers, set up in the government offices, and promulgated among the people.[41] If the law is not uniform, there will be misfortune for the holder of the state . . . [42]

It is well established that the Yi Dynasty (1392-1910) in Korea was founded with the support of the Confucian-scholar class of the preceding Koryo dynasty, and that the values of the Neo-Confucianist, Chu-shi (1130-1200 A.D.), defined and informed the administrative structure of the new dynastic order.[43] Yet, in spite of the traditional Confucian rejection of Legalist ideas, Korea saw a pronounced development and careful codification of laws under the kings of the Yi Dynasty. Understanding this apparent inconsistency requires a brief examination of the history of written law in Korea. This examination reveals that the apparent inconsistency represents, in fact, a persistent tension between concepts of Legalism and Confucian ideology that may have ultimately resulted in a balance of power between a highly developed Confucian bureaucracy and a legalistic monarchy.

---

[40] Hahm, *Korean Political Tradition*, *supra* note 5, pp. 42-43.

[41] Fung, *Chinese Philosophy*, *supra* note 3, p. 322 (quoting from the *Han Fei-tzu*, ch. 38, *chuan* 16 (Legalist doctrine)).

[42] *Id.* (quoting from the *HanFeitzu*, ch. 45, *chuan* 15 (Legalist doctrine)).

[43] Han, Woo Keun, *The History of Korea* (Seoul: Eul-Yoo Publishing Co., 1970), p. 203 [hereinafter *History of Korea*].

The history of written law in Korea reaches as far back as Ancient Choson (4th century B.C.). As the first of a number of tribal leagues that developed on the peninsula,[44] Ancient Choson represents the emergence of a social order existing above the level of the communal tribe. It is significant to the history of Korean law that this increasing complexity took place contemporaneously with the Warring States period in China.[45] The reader will recall that it was during this period that the Legalist schools emerged. Since it is during this period that Korea also first began to feel the pervasive influence of events in China, it is not surprising that the first examples of written law in Korean history would also appear at this time. Looking to the laws themselves, the Legalist influence is apparent. The scant records of Ancient Choson mention eight laws, three of which have come down to us in recorded form: murderers were to be punished by immediate execution; the victim's family was to be compensated in grain by the murderer's family; and thieves were to serve as slaves to the owners of the property they stole.[46] What is important to note in this earliest record of written Korean law is that the main thrust is to declare what is to be the *punishment* for the transgression cited.

The Three Kingdoms Period (1st century B.C. - 10th century A.D.) saw the development of the tribal leagues into broadly organized kingdoms.[47] With this further increase in social complexity came an increase in written laws, organized bureaucracies, and centralized monarchical power. For example, in Koguryo, the first kingdom to emerge during this period, a "regular administrative system governing through laws and decrees" was established under the reign of Sosurim (r. 371-384).[48] In the Paekche kingdom, the second kingdom to emerge, civil and military affairs were placed under the control of a graded system of officials.[49] And finally, with the founding of Silla, the title of *maripkan*, a word of Korean origin meaning "great chieftain" was replaced by the Chinese title *wang*, mean-

---

[44] *Id.*, p. 12.
[45] *See id.*, p. 12,14.
[46] *Id.*, p. 17.
[47] *Id.*, p. 41. The three kingdoms are Koguryo, Paekche, and Silla.
[48] *Id.*, p. 52.
[49] *Id.*, pp. 55-56.

ing "king." Under the first of these Silla kings, Pophung-wang (514-539), various laws were promulgated and a government administration based on those laws was created.[50] It cannot be doubted that these developments are highly consistent with the Chinese Legalist prescription for 'government by law,' since the application of power by the monarch through the utilization of laws is an idea very much at the heart of that philosophy. Similar to developments in China, the advent of administrative systems in Korea, based as they were on laws and decrees, had the prescribed effect of subjugating clan and tribal leaders to the ascending monarchy.[51]

The following Koryo period (936-1392) saw the unification of the three kingdoms under a single dynasty. This, of course, necessitated a unification of the previous bodies of law. However, no such attempt was made until just prior to the end the Koryo Dynasty. At that time, the scholar Chong Mong-ju completed a compilation of the entire body of laws produced during the Three Kingdoms and Koryo periods. This compilation was modeled on the codes of the Chinese Yuan and Ming dynasties.[52]

With the founding of the Yi Dynasty in 1392, many changes were made to the numerous laws that had been compiled by Chong and a new codification was accordingly undertaken by Chong To-on in 1395.[53] Being the work of a single scholar, however, this compilation was lacking in completeness, and in 1397 King T'aejo (r. 1392-98) ordered a comprehensive compilation of laws and decrees promulgated since the reign of King U (late Koryo). Distributed throughout the kingdom, the compilation at last provided a complete code of laws on which the government officials of the time could "base their work."[54] Unfortunately, this new compilation, which came to be known as the *Six Codes* (for the six ministries through which it was ultimately administered),[55] contained numerous inconsistencies and contradictions due to the fact that many of the laws it contained had been formulated at different points in time through-

[50] *Id.*, p. 57.
[51] *Id.*, p. 51.
[52] *Id.*, p. 216
[53] *Id.*
[54] *Id.*, p. 217.
[55] *Id.*, p. 216. The Six Ministries were the Ministries of Personnel, Revenue, Rites, War, Justice and Public Works. *Id.*, p. 229.

out the previous dynasties and under varying political circumstances.[56]

King Sejong (r.1418-50), revered in Korean history for his devotion to social and cultural advancement, and credited for the development of the Korean alphabet, established in 1424 an institute for the specific purpose of unifying the various sources of law.[57] Due to a revised method of organization that ordered the laws by subject (rather than the separate reigns of the kings who had produced them), followed by a reconciliation of the laws within a given subject area, a consistent code of laws was finally completed and promulgated in 1470 under the reign of King Songjong.[58] This codification, known as the *Gyeongguk Daejeon* (Grand Code for Managing the Nation) became the basis of all Korean law until modernization reforms were undertaken in the late 19th century just prior to Japanese colonization.[59]

Such fervent work on the part of the Yi Dynasty can hardly be taken as a case of the monarchy simply doing its job. In a society supposedly based on the Confucian concept of the sage-king who should deplore a resort to laws, why would a king even consider the development of a unified code of laws to be his job? In spite of the Confucian leanings underpinning the administrative development of Yi Dynasty Korea, it may be argued that the development of legal codes by the monarchy in pre-modern Korea reflected an effort on the part of the monarchy to take hold of the reigns of kingship in a manner quite similar to that espoused by the Chinese Legalists. Thus, while it is often said the Yi Dynasty was a Confucian-based dynasty, it may be more accurate to say that although the bureaucracy of the Yi Dynasty relied on a Confucian ideology for its legitimacy, the Dynasty itself did not. A heavy emphasis on the codification of laws, the legitimation and maintenance of power through those laws, and the nature of the laws themselves being that of severe punishment, supports such an interpretation.

However, it can also be argued that these (Chinese) Legalistic tendencies were kept in check by a Confucian ideology that had gained a foothold in the governing of the state due to its formative role in the

[56] *Id.*, p. 217
[57] *Id.*
[58] *Id.*
[59] *Id.*

founding of the dynasty. Such an interpretation of the relationship between the ruler and a Confucian bureaucracy is not without precedent. Fung describes Confucian, Mohist, and Taoist political theories as discussing government from the point of view of the people, while the Legalists discussed it wholly from the point of view of the ruler.[60] This interpretation of the relationship between the Confucians and the Chinese Legalists suggests a similar relationship between the bureaucracy and the monarchy of Yi Dynasty Korea. While the development and application of strict legal codes may indicate a propensity for Chinese Legalist ideas on the part of the Korean monarchy, adherence to and insistence upon the Confucian values of *li* reflects a response to that monarchical power on the part of the bureaucracy. Were it not for the Confucians, the growth of monarchical power based on punitive laws may very well have gone permanently unchecked in Yi Dynasty Korea.

With the Neo-Confucian transformation of Korean society under the Yi Dynasty, Confucian ideals became fully integrated into the Korean sense of social order.[61] Since the use of laws represented nothing more than the arm by which the king was to apply and maintain his power, the out-right rejection of laws, on the ground that they were barbaric and inhuman, effectively blocked the growth of absolute monarchical power. This was achieved by an appeal to the preferred values of the larger social system. A strictly Confucian bureaucracy that rejected the use of punitive laws (and hence *all* laws in their view) was thus able to keep a potentially burgeoning monarchy in check. A proper and humane king would not turn to his laws as a means of maintaining social order. Rather, the principles of *li* were to be obeyed, *especially* by the king. An example of the means by which this Confucian check on the monarchy was realized may be seen in the fact that the bureaucracy took it upon itself to attempt an inculcation of Confucian values in the king through regular education in the Confucian classics.[62] All of these factors indicate that the existence of

---

[60] Fung, *Chinese Philosophy*, *supra* note 3, p. 312.

[61] For a full description of this transformation, see Martina Deuchler, *The Confucian Transformation of Korea: A Study of Society and Ideology* (Cambridge, MA: Harvard University Press, 1992).

[62] For an account of the Confucian training of the crown prince, see Jahyun Kim Haboush, "The Education of the Yi Crown Prince: A Study in Confucian Pedagogy," in

a strongly Confucian bureaucracy avoided the rise of an unfettered absolute power resting in the monarchy in Yi Dynasty Korea.[63]

In a purely social context, the legal consciousness that subsequently arose out of the tension between Chinese-style Legalism and the ideals of Confucianism is one that came to distrust any system of social order that has at its foundation a reliance on laws. The legalism of the monarchy led to the development and promulgation of laws and their codification, while Confucian ideology considered a reliance on those laws to be inhuman. The inherent conflict of Confucianism and Chinese Legalism, and the fact that both played a major role in the development of the traditional Korean socio-political system therefore suggests an explanation for the apparent conflict in Korean attitudes toward the prevailing view of desirable social values and the development and application of laws.

This *a priori* tension over the reliance on *any* system of laws may serve to explain the source of Korean apprehension toward the Western sense of legality. Because the concept and function of punishment is of course an accepted and integral part of the Western legal tradition, the Western tradition is immediately associated with the kind of punitive legalism espoused by the Chinese Legalists and it is thereby rejected on the grounds that the Western system is fundamentally opposed to the preferred system of social order. Furthermore, since the presumption on both sides of the Confucian/Legalist debate was that punitive laws (and, hence, *all* laws) were an inseparable function of absolute power, the existence and use of laws is taken to be representative of the existence, or at least desire for, domination. Hahm points out that according to the traditional Korean perspective,

> An attempt to define one's relationship with others in terms of law and legal rights is usually considered a prelude to war. The attempt is to secede from the 'decent' lifestyle to another much more warlike and conflict-dynamic life style, characterized by

---

Wm. Theodore de Bary and JaHyun Haboush (eds.), *The Rise of Neo-Confucianism in Korea* (New York: Columbia University Press, 1985), p. 161.

[63] It is well known that the history of Yi Dynasty Korea, similar to the histories of most monarchies, is rife with examples of the persistent wrangling between the Confucian bureaucracy and the throne. See generally, Han, *History of Korea, supra* note 43, pp. 203-357.

individual defiance and desire to dominate other men and Nature.[64]

Thus, in both the Confucian and Chinese Legalist view, absolute power and law have always meant one and the same thing. Where there is an acceptance of laws, there must be an acceptance of absolute power. As such, the Western system, filled with a seemingly endless proliferation of laws, is to the conventional Korean worldview highly suspect.

Of course, this association of the Western legal tradition with notions reminiscent of Chinese Legalism misses a very critical distinction between the two bodies of thought. As previously illustrated, the salient feature of Chinese Legalism was an emphasis on absolute power with the use of punitive laws as the means by which that power was to be acquired and maintained. In this context, laws are used to promote absolute power. However, significant developments in the Western legal tradition regarding the role of law have given law the additional function of *preventing* the ascension of absolute power. I am referring, of course, to the development of Constitutionalism. In the Constitutional approach to power and government, the separation of the centers of power, and the guarantee of certain rights vis-à-vis the ruler, produces a system of laws which in themselves aim at the prevention of the abuse of law. Thus, it may be said that in dealing with the problem of the abusive or unjust law, the two systems took radically different approaches. While the Confucian system came to *reject* laws altogether as an expression of the absence of any true justice, exchanging them instead for an insistence upon the fundamental role of social relationships, the Western system *retains* law but turns it on itself as a means of tempering its tendencies toward excess. This distinction, whereby law itself is used to check the advent of unjust law, makes the Western conception of law, taken as a whole, quite different from that put forth by the Chinese Legalists. As such, a comparison of the East Asian legal tradition with that of the West based entirely on notions of 'legalism' presents a false dichotomy that can only lead to persistent misconceptions of both the East Asian and Western legal traditions.

The table below summarizes the distinctions raised in the foregoing discussion between Chinese Legalism, Confucianism, and Western

---

[64] Hahm, Pyong Choon, "The Impact of Traditional Legacies on the Contemporary Judicial Process in Korea," in Hahm, *Korean Jurisprudence, supra* note 5, p. 249.

'legalism' as they deal with the relationship between absolute power and laws. A simple comparison of the values supported by Confucianism and the Western legal tradition shows that while the 'Rejection (Acceptance) of Laws' provides a clear point of divergence between the two systems, the 'Rejection of Absolute Power' nonetheless provides a point of commonality.

Relationship between Laws and Absolute Power in Chinese Legalism, Confucianism, and Western 'Legalism'		
Chinese Legalism	**Confucianism**	**Western 'Legalism'**
Acceptance of Absolute Power	Rejection of Absolute Power	Rejection of Absolute Power
Acceptance of laws as the means by which absolute power is exercised and maintained	Rejection of laws as nothing more than the tool of the absolute ruler	Acceptance of laws as the means by which absolute rule is limited

IV FOUNDATIONAL PRINCIPLES OF NATURAL LAW AND CONFUCIANISM

The existence of both divergence and commonality between the major schools of East Asian legal philosophy and the dominant trends in the Western legal tradition on the question of absolute power and the abuse of law should alert us to the possibility that a distinction between the two systems of thought may exist at a level deeper than concerns over the meaning of 'legality.' I suggest here that this distinction may lie in the foundational presumptions that inform the Positive Law/Natural Law and Chinese Legalist/Confucian debates over the relationship between law and morality. It should be clear from the discussion above that the Chinese Legalist tradition shares an almost one-to-one correspondence with the conception of law espoused by the positivists of Western legal philosophy, whereby that which may be truly referred to as 'law' can only be that which is the command of the sovereign. The most apposite representatives of this position are, of course, Hobbes, and his conception of law as the decrees of the absolute monarch,[65] and Austin, with his theory of command and punishment as the essence of law.[66] On this view of law, then, it may be said that the debates over law and morality in Western and East Asian jurisprudence overlap.

However, it is in Western conceptions of natural law as they pertain to the positivist position and the Confucian rejection of Chinese Legalism where the histories diverge. While it is clear that both the Natural Law tradition and Confucian thinking stand in opposition to concepts of purely positive law, they come to vastly different conclusions as to the relationship between law and morality. In the Natural Law tradition, concepts of law and morality lead to a sense of 'higher law' whereby some form of superior or transcendental law is utilized to place a moral limit on state power and its reliance on positive law. Confucian thought, on the other hand, in its reaction to notions of law as the punitive commands of the ruler, be they just or unjust, simply rejects law altogether. This divergence can be explained as an outcome of the fundamentally different points of origin taken by the two systems of thought in their respective expositions of the relationship between law and society.

A. Natural Law and the Origins of Society

A dominant theme in the Natural Law tradition when it attempts to explain the role of law in society is the conception of 'pre-social' man.[67] According to Cairns, this idea can be traced all the way back to the Greeks:

> [I]n the effort to find a constant element in the apparent world of flux . . . we find Democritus, the originator of the atomic theory, taking the position that color and taste exist by convention and that reality is to be found in the atom and the void. It was inevitable that the same problem should arise with respect to law. It received its classic exposition in chapter

---

[65] *See generally*, Thomas Hobbes, *Leviathan* (1651).

[66] *See generally,* John Austin, *The Province of Jurisprudence Determined* (1832).

[67] *Accord,* Michael Freeden, *Rights* (Minneapolis: University of Minnesota Press, 1991), p. 34 (discussing the assumption of the "pre-sociality" of natural rights).

> seven of Book Five of the Nichomachean Ethics, where Aristotle drew a distinction between the rules of natural justice which have the same validity everywhere and do not depend on our accepting them or not, and rules of conventional justice which in the first instance may be settled in one way or the other indifferently.[68]

Herein lies the beginning of a transcendent concept of law that lies somewhere beyond the temporal exigencies of society. What is important to note, however, is not so much the introduction of transcendence into questions of law, for even the Confucian reliance on rules of *li* can be said to lay hold of a set of principles that are taken to be universal and timeless in nature. What is important, rather, is that in this early stage of Western thought on law and society, that which is held to be transcendent is found to lie *outside* the notion of society.

This framework is picked up by practically every prominent Natural Law thinker forward.[69] For Cicero,[70] law begins with the *lex caelestis*. He argues that "law is not a product of human thought, nor is it any enactment of peoples, but something eternal which rules the whole universe by its wisdom . . . ."[71] In Aquinas' time, concepts of natural law were identified by the Fathers of the Church with the law of God.[72] In this way, natural law was viewed as the unchanging *source* of positive law.[73] When positive law was contrary to natural law, or when it opposed the social ideals of the Church, the idea of a Primitive State was posited in which "a pure law of nature operated unimpaired; unjust laws and institutions

---

[68] Cairns, *supra* note 1, pp. 25-26; *see also* Freeden, *supra* note 69, p. 25 ("Natural rights, in their original form, may be traced back to natural law and natural law transports us back to the Greeks.").

[69] *See* Cairns, *supra* note 1, p. 26.

[70] Referring to Cicero as a "natural law thinker" is of course problematic since in his view three kinds of law operate in the world. These are the *lex caelestis*, the *uis naturae*, and the *uis vulgus* (referring to the idea of law as that which decrees in written form whatever it wishes, either by command or prohibition.) *See* Cairns, *supra* note 1, pp. 135-42. Cicero's thought therefore includes notions of transcendental law, "natural" law, and positive law.

[71] Cairns, *supra* note 1, p. 135.

[72] *Id.*, p. 165.

[73] *Id.*

could therefore be explained as due to Original Sin."[74] Thus, government and institutions were viewed as something *not* belonging to the original nature of man.

Perhaps the most well known example of this 'pre-social' approach to the justification of 'natural' rights is that of Locke's social contract. In his theories on the origin of the State and the retention of natural rights by the individual, Locke relies on a distinction between man-in-nature and man-in-society. He defines the 'natural' condition of human beings to be one that is pre-social. It is a "state of perfect freedom to order their actions, and dispose of their possessions and persons as they think fit, within the bounds of the law of Nature, without asking leave or depending upon the will of any other man."[75] In order to avoid the insecurities of this state of nature, however, "men unit[ed] themselves into commonwealths, and put[] themselves under government."[76] According to the Lockean conception of natural and social man, then, "all men are in a state of nature, and remain so until they make themselves members of a political society."[77] Thus, in support of his theory of natural rights retaining their legitimacy in organized society, Locke makes use of a "vital shift from pre-political society to political society."[78]

Further examples of this reliance on a concept of pre-social man can be found in the writings of Rousseau and the modern contractarian John Rawls. Rousseau's approach to social morality invokes the idea of "noble savages" living free and independent lives who enter into social relationships based solely on their individual interests.[79] As for Rawls, his conceptions of law and morality make the pre-social, competitive and atomistic nature of man an express condition of man's "original position."[80]

It should be apparent from the foregoing that, in the broadest sense, Natural Law doctrines take as a foundational principle conceptions of

---

[74] *Id.*

[75] *Id.*, p. 339 (citing Locke)

[76] *Id.*, p. 351.

[77] *Id.*, p. 341 (citing Locke)

[78] *Id.*, p. 351.

[79] *See* Peerenboom, *supra* note 3, p. 126.

[80] *Id.*, pp. 126-127.

man and society that place man's original nature as one that exists outside the perceived artifice of society. That is, society is viewed not as something that is a natural expression of man, but rather, man *leaves* nature to *form* society. Natural rights are carried over into society because they are "not the product of any social artifice, historical growth or political contrivance."[81] Rather, "political societies [are] *created* for the very purpose of ensuring the recognition and enforcement of natural rights."[82] Notions of justice are therefore grounded in man's extra-social existence. Any attempt to interfere with such universal and absolute principles, "would be — it was assumed — potentially catastrophic for both individual and society."[83] In our comparison with the Confucian view of law, what is important to recognize here is that in the Natural Law doctrines of the West nature and society are viewed as two different things, and that *natural man* is therefore not *social man*.

B. Confucian Legal Philosophy and the Foundations of Society

Confucius is often viewed as a natural law advocate. Such prominent scholars as Needham, Duyvendak, and Bodde have all portrayed Confucian theory as a variant on Natural Law ideas.[84] Undoubtedly, this is due to the Confucian emphasis on virtue as an organizing principle of society. However, the classification of Confucian thought as a form of natural law theory overlooks the point raised above regarding the Confucian view of law and society. As indicated, Confucian thought altogether *rejects* law as an essential organizing principle for social order. This fact alone makes it difficult to reconcile Confucian thought with a notion of an extra-social imperative justifying the requirements of social order, which is at the heart of Western Natural Law doctrines.

In this regard, rather than viewing society as once removed from nature, whereby man leaves nature to enter society, Confucianism views

---

[81] Freeden, *supra* note 69, p. 27.

[82] *Id.* (emphasis added).

[83] *Id.*

[84] *See* Peerenboom, *supra* note 3, p. 118 (citing Joseph Needham, *Science and Civilization in China*, Vol. 2 (Cambridge, England: University Press, 1954); J. J. L. Duyvendak, *The Book of Lord Shang* (London: A. Probsthain, 1928); Derk Bodde, "Evidence for the 'Laws of Nature' in Chinese Thought," *Harvard Journal of Asiatic Studies*, vol. 20 (1979)).

society itself as an *expression* of nature. Hall and Ames recognized this theme in Confucian thinking (though outside the context of a discussion on law) when they described the Confucian sense of social being whereby "'sociality' is at the very root of existence."[85]

While the Western tradition speaks of man's 'natural state' as being his existence in nature, attaching thus a certain artificiality to man-in-society, Confucianism instead draws a distinction between human beings as biological species and human beings as social organism.[86] That is, when Confucius speaks of the "five-relationships" he is not speaking of them as relationships that come into being when man enters into society.[87] The five-relationships are instead the very structure out of which society emerges. Hence, one's natural humanity is *found* by living consistently with the natural principles upon which society has emerged. This is in stark contrast to the Natural Law tradition where law is regarded as having an extra-human origin.[88] Peerenboom explains:

> [W]here many contractarians and morality of law proponents see ahistorical individuals in competition with each other, Confucius sees persons bound together by deep historical roots grounded in the traditional li understood to include the full range of social customs, mores, and norms embodied in the complex relationships, organizations, and institutions of society.[89]

As an explicit example of this point, it is interesting to note that Locke, the quintessential contractarian, finds in the law-making function the single element which *distinguishes* the power of the state from that of

---

[85] Hall & Ames, *supra* note 3, p. 153.

[86] Peerenboom, *supra* note 3, p. 128.

[87] The "five relationships" are: King and Subject, Parent and Child, Husband and Wife, Master and Servant, and Friend-to-Friend. It is important to note that despite a suggestion of hierarchy in some of these relationships, and while the distribution of decision-making authority may in fact be defined in Confucian thought by the relative social position of the constituents, the relationships nonetheless carry with them a view to their function as being fundamentally symbiotic. That is, each member of the foundational relationship has obligations to the other.

[88] *Id.*, p. 170.

[89] Peerenboom, *supra* note 3, p. 128.

"a father over his children, a master over his servant, a husband over his wife, and a lord over his slave."[90] For Locke, law stands at the dividing line between natural man and society. On the one side, we have the essence of man with his absolute freedoms, and on the other, we have society and its interference in those freedoms. For Confucius, since man is *already* in his natural state *within* society, to say that law comes naturally from some source *outside* of society is to speak, quite literally, of *nothing*. That is, there is no nature 'outside' of society from whence a Supreme Law can filter down into the artifices of man's conveniences, since society itself is included in *all* that is nature. It is not surprising, then, to find that a Confucian view of law sees it as nothing more than a tool for the control of society at its extremes, and in so doing, finds it less than adequate when compared to the observation of the rules of interpersonal relationship, since it is these that exist as the basis of society and inform its very fabric.

V THE PROBLEM OF THE UNJUST LAW

With this last point in mind, a comparative analysis of the problem of the unjust law in East Asian and Western jurisprudence is at last possible. It should be clear from the foregoing that the two systems take very different approaches to dealing with unjust law, or as the progenitor of such law, the unjust ruler. Plainly put, the Western response is to set law against law. As the table in the previous section indicates, the problem of the unjust law in Western jurisprudence is dealt with by calling forth the notion of a higher law that will limit the power of an absolute ruler. As the practical expression of this notion, constitutionalism serves as a check on the prospect of unjust laws promulgated by an absolute ruler. The concepts supporting this constitutionalism find their basis in notions of natural law. That is, constitutionalism represents a body of law that appeals to a higher moral order by which the power of the rule-maker is checked through the very laws created in its name. In the natural rights tradition, an appeal to rights arising out of man's natural state *outside* of society is used to check the excesses of law *within* society. In this we have the classic principle of constitutionalism by which the power of the state is limited by the naturally found rights of the extra-social individual.

---

[90] Cairns, *supra* note 1, p. 339.

For the Confucians, all law is essentially inhuman since it is not part of that which forms the essence of man, namely his relationships with others. Law is the tool of all who would rule by something other than *li*, and as such can never be the conduit of any form of 'justice.' As mentioned earlier, notions of justice (*i*) are associated with the natural foundations of society *li*. Given that the Confucians embrace *li* as the organizing principle of society and reject law as that which interferes with the true emergence of society, it is easy to see how the Confucians avoid any association between notions of justice and a social order based on law.

Nonetheless, this does not answer the problem of what is prescribed in Confucian thinking for the eventuality of unjust law. However, a closer look reveals that it is this very rejection of a notion of laws having anything to do with the true ordering of society, that Confucianism sets out to contain the excesses of law. Rather than setting law against law, as in the West, it may be said that the Confucians set *li* against law. As mentioned above, the Confucian ruler is schooled from the earliest age in the Confucian classics. It is expected that any ruler who follows these precepts faithfully will be living in accordance with nature and therefore in accordance with the foundations of society. Ruling outside of these tenets presents the prospect of running afoul of nature. In a society that sees itself standing firmly on the natural principles of interpersonal relationship, it is not difficult to imagine that the violation of these principles may have presented to the mind of the transgressor a very real sense that his entire existence may be teetering on the brink of destruction should the *li* be ignored. In the same way, perhaps, that a Western mind steeped in Judeo-Christian notions of Divine natural law may have felt a sense of dread over the possibility of an unpredictable retribution for transgressions of the Divine Command, it is possible that the Confucian mind felt a similar dread over the potential disintegration of his society should the natural principles of *li* be violated. With this in mind, it is possible to posit that the Confucian system of thought may have provided just as effective a deterrent to the possibility of unjust law as that presented by constitutionalism in the West.

CONCLUSION

Although the Natural Law/Positive Law debate in Western jurisprudence and the Confucian/Chinese Legalist debate in East Asian legal philosophy overlap on concepts of 'law as punishment,' they wholly diverge on the question of law and justice. This is because the schools of thought that represent the dominant argument for morality in law and society within the two traditions begin from very different precepts. While proponents of the Natural Law doctrine in the West typically start with *man-in-nature*, in contrast to *man-in-society*, as the source of natural law, Confucian thought views *man-in-society* as man's natural origin. These very different assumptions about the original state of man lead to very different conceptions about the place of law in society. For Western thinkers, natural law provides a check on the excesses of positive law, thereby reducing the possibility for the advent of unjust laws. For the Confucians, the rejection of laws altogether and an emphasis on a 'humanizing' set of social principles that are the very architecture upon which *society-as-nature* stands provide a formidable deterrent to the unfettered reign of an unjust ruler. Thus, in spite of the fact that the systems begin from very different premises, they nonetheless provide a means by which law that is not consistent with the requirements of 'justice' is avoided.

Certainly, both systems have had their successes and failures. Whichever society we choose to focus on at any given point in time will undoubtedly provide us with plenty of cases in which the ideal did not hold. It is not my purpose, nor is it within the scope of this study, to discuss how effectively each system 'really worked.' Such discussions are only concerned with the relative worth of each system and soon lead to the question, "Which one is better?" The underlying assumption of such a question is that we must ultimately choose to align ourselves with one system or the other. This is very far from the direction of this study. If anything, it is hoped that the foregoing discussion illustrates that any claim that notions of law in Western and East Asian legal philosophy are diametrically opposed, or that they are essentially the same, presents a far too simplistic assessment of the relationship between Western and East Asian jurisprudence. In a discussion of two systems of thought whose motivations and goals are similar while their methods and founding norms are significantly divergent, where do the words 'same' and 'different' fit with the overall assessment of that relationship? Thus it may be said that although civilization in the Western tradition reaches its height by *setting itself apart from and rising above* an *orderless* Nature, and in the Confucian tradition society reaches its height by *becoming the perfect expression of* an *ordered* Nature, both traditions obviously agree that civilization reaches its height by the achievement of order. The test of our humanity then, in either tradition, is our ability to accommodate the truth of either views of man and nature in the service a just society. That is, fundamental differences in the conception of what are the essential qualities of Nature and Society obviously lead to very different prescriptions by which a just society is to be attained. Nonetheless, in both systems the aspiration remains the same — the creation of a state of humanity that is free of injustice.

THE NEO-CONFUCIAN THEORY OF LI, THE GOODNESS OF HUMAN NATURE, AND THE NATURAL LAW
Peter P. Cvek

One of the hallmarks of orthodox Confucianism is the doctrine of the goodness of human nature. Although initially advanced by Mencius (372-289 BCE) in the late fourth century BCE, the acceptance of this position was not without opposition. Mencius, in fact, contrasted his own belief in the basic goodness of human nature with those who maintained that human nature is neither good nor bad, that human nature can become either good or bad, and that human nature is basically bad.[1] Despite Mencius's advocacy of the goodness of human nature, a century later Hsün-tzu (313-238 BCE) declared that human nature is basically bad, and later Yang Hsiung (53 BCE-18 CE) claimed that human nature was a mixture of good and bad. As observed by A.C. Graham, "this profoundly troubling issue, a threat to the foundations of Confucian moralism, continued to be discussed, urgently and fruitlessly, even at the times when Confucians showed least interest in philosophical abstractions."[2] For example, during the T'ang dynasty, Han Yu (768-824 CE) argued that there are three grades of human nature: good, intermediate, and bad; his disciple Li Ao agreed with Mencius; while Tu Mu agreed with Hsün-tzu.[3] The debate continued well into the Sung dynasty. Chou Tun-yi (1017-1073 CE) treated human nature as a mixture of good and bad. Chang Tsai (1020-1077 CE) and Ch'eng Hao (1032-1085 CE) approximated the Mencian doctrine, but insisted that while it is good to act according to one's nature, the term *good* could not properly be ascribed to human nature itself. It was not until Cheng Yi (1033-1107 CE) and especially Chu Hsi (1130-1200 CE) that the Mencian theory of the goodness of human nature achieved the status of Confucian orthodoxy.

Since the doctrine of the goodness of human nature has been a part of

---

[1] Angus C. Graham, "What was new in the Cheng-Chu Theory of Human Nature?" in *Chu Hsi and Neo-Confucianism*, edited by Wing-tsit Chan (Honolulu: University of Hawaii Press, 1986), p. 138.

[2] Ibid., p. 138.

[3] Ibid., p. 138.

Confucian thought for so long, it is easy to forget that the general acceptance of this position came only after a millennium and a half long debate. The end of this controversy undoubtedly represents a significant moment in the history of Confucian philosophy. The purpose of this paper is to investigate the conceptual framework that made this resolution possible. The paper is divided into three parts. In part one, I will examine and attempt to define the concept of *li* (principle), the central doctrinal innovation of Sung dynasty Neo-Confucianism. In part two, I will review the contemporary debate over the correct interpretation of this concept by focusing on whether it is appropriate to view *li* as playing a role analogous to that played by the idea of *natural law* in the western philosophical tradition. Finally, in part three, I will show how the concept of *li*, understood as a principle which is both transcendent and immanent, provides the metaphysical foundation for establishing the goodness of human nature, albeit in a manner beyond that envisioned by Mencius. Moreover, I will argue that this metaphysical foundation is best understood as similar to the metaphysical structure which is found in the ethics of natural law in the western philosophical tradition, especially as found in the philosophy of Thomas Aquinas.

THE THEORY OF LI

The key to the Neo-Confucian defense of the goodness of human nature lies in the concept of *Li*, typically translated as "principle" or "pattern". Sung dynasty Neo-Confucianism is often called the "School of Principle" (*Li-hsüeh*), so there is little doubt about the importance of this element. Nevertheless, there is considerable controversy surrounding the correct interpretation of this concept. The following discussion will focus on the thought of Chu Hsi as the culmination and synthesis of Sung Neo-Confucianism, although references will be made to the thought of Ch'eng Yi and Ch'eng Hao when necessary. My immediate aim is simply to ascertain the manner in which *li* functions as a principle of explanation within the Neo-Confucian world-view.

According to A.C. Graham, the word *li* is used as a noun ("principle") and as a verb ("to put in order").[4] The character is written with the "jade"

---

[4] Angus C. Graham, *Two Chinese Philosophers* (LaSalle, Illinois: Open Court Press, 1992), p. 8.

radical, and it has long been assumed that its primary meaning as a noun is "veins in jade," as a verb "to dress jade," an etymology taken for granted by Sung philosophers. The Ch'eng brothers never provided an explicit definition, but in later writings of the Sung School, we find the following description: "If we exhaust the principles in the things of the world, it will be found that a thing must have a reason why it is as it is and a rule to which it should conform, which is meant by principle."[5] *Li* can thus be understood in at least two ways. First, it can designate the *reason why* something is what it is. Second, it can refer to a *rule* with which an activity is in conformity. The following passages illustrate the use of *li* as a principle of explanation, such that to understand the *li* of a thing is to understand why the thing is what it is.

> All things have principles, for example, that by which fire is hot and that by which water is cold ... There is a single principle in outside things and in the self; as soon as 'that' is understood 'this' becomes clear. This is the way to unite external and internal. The scholar should understand everything, at one extreme the height of heaven and thickness of earth, at the other that by which a single thing is as it is.[6]

Thus to understand a thing's principle is to understand that which makes it be what it is. Moreover, understanding is a way of uniting the internal and the external. This implies that knowledge is a kind of correspondence between the knowing subject and the known object, which is mediated by principle, the immediate object of genuine knowledge.

The sense of a *rule* to which natural activities conform is seen in the following passage: "It is a constant principle that a tree flowers in spring and fades in autumn. As for perpetual flowering there is no such principle."[7] In this case, the rule is descriptive. Other passages indicate that *li* is also used in a normative sense to prescribe what actions ought to occur, if they are to be in conformity with a rule. For example:

> That this man stayed at his side and guarded him till dawn; how could he leave him and go home himself? This is as it should be as a matter of principle.

[5] Cited by Graham, *Two Chinese Philosophers*, p. 8.
[6] Cited by Graham, *Two Chinese Philosophers*, p. 8.
[7] Ibid., p. 9.

> Not to be resentful against heaven and not to blame man is as it should be in principle.

> That the ruler is superior to the minister is a constant principle of the Empire. Consideration of others is a principle which exists of itself.[8]

While it is clear that *li* is intended to serve as a principle of explanation of some kind, *li* is also used in a more substantive sense to refer to a constituent element of things in the phenomenal world. Chu Hsi makes it clear that everything which exists or may exist is said to be a combination of *li* (principle) and *ch'i* (material force). Thus we are told that:

> The nature of man and things is nothing but principle and cannot be spoken of in terms of integration and disintegration. That which integrates to produce life and disintegrates to produce death is only material force...As to principle, fundamentally it does not exist or cease to exist because of such integration or disintegration. As there is a certain principle, there is the material force corresponding to it and as this material force integrates in a particular instance, its principle is also endowed in that instance.[9]

The precise nature of the relationship between principle and material force is a subject of considerable dispute and will be examined in more detail below. Before taking up that discussion, however, the concept of *li* needs to be placed within a greater metaphysical context.

Moving from the microcosm to the macrocosm, just as every particular thing has its respective principle, Heaven and Earth taken as a whole must have a principle which embraces and explains the totality of what is. This all embracing principle is called the Supreme Ultimate or *T'ai Chi*. The Supreme Ultimate is nothing but principle, yet, it is that which encompasses the principles of all things. "The Supreme Ultimate is merely the principle of heaven and earth and the myriad things…With respect to heaven and earth, there is the Supreme Ultimate in each and every one

---

[8] Ibid., p. 8-9.

[9] Wing-tsit Chan, *A Source Book of Chinese Philosophy* (Princeton: Princeton University Press, 1963), pp. 637-8.

of them. Before heaven and earth existed, there was assuredly this principle."[10] Although there is only one Supreme Ultimate, each thing is endowed with it and each thing possesses it in its entirety. As Chu Hsi explains, "this is similar to the fact that there is only one moon in the sky but when its light is scattered upon rivers and lakes, it can be seen everywhere. It cannot be said that the moon has been split."[11] As interpreted by Wing-tsit Chan, the Supreme Ultimate is simply the principle of the highest good which is wholly present in each and every person or thing.[12] Commenting on this same passage, Fung Yu-lan concludes that "the Supreme Ultimate is very much like what Plato called the Idea of the Good, or what Aristotle called God."[13]

Many commentators, including Fung Yu-lan, Chan Wing-tsit, and Carson Chang, have noted the similarities between the thought of Chu Hsi and that advanced by Plato and Aristotle.[14] Chu Hsi's insistence on the unity of *li* and *ch'i* in concrete things does compare favorably with Aristotle's doctrine of hylomorphism. Chu Hsi would also seem to agree that *li* is that which explains what something is, while matter is the explanation of particularity and plurality.[15] Moreover, as Chang observes, both Aristotle and Chu Hsi assert that "an entity exists which imparts motion but is itself unmoved."[16] This is God according to Aristotle and Heaven (as reason/principle) according to Chu Hsi. Yet, Chang adds, in so far as Chu Hsi grounds all meaning and value on the eternal and unchanging principle, which is logically independent of changeable particulars, his thought is reminiscent of the Platonic theory of Forms.[17]

---

[10] Ibid., p. 638.

[11] Ibid., p. 638.

[12] Chan, *Source Book*, p. 638.

[13] Fung Yu-lan, *A History of Chinese Philosophy* (Princeton University Press, 1953), volume 2, p. 537.

[14] Chang, for example, concludes that as "a student of the phenomenal world [Chu Hsi] was an Aristotelian; but yet he was also a Platonist in his idealism." Carson Chang, *The Development of Neo-Confucian Thought* (New York: Bookman Associates, 1957), p. 254.

[15] See Wing-tsit Chan, *Chu Hsi: Life and Thought* (The Chinese University of Hong Kong, 1987), p. 111-112, for a decidedly Aristotelian interpretation of principle and material force.

[16] Chang, The *Development of Neo-Confucian Thought*, p. 255.

[17] Ibid., p. 254.

Other commentators, however, have categorically rejected this comparison as a metaphysical distortion of Chu Hsi's naturalistic philosophy. Joseph Needham, for instance, argues extensively against any Platonic-Aristotelian interpretation of Chu Hsi's philosophy.

> It is true that form was the factor of individuation, that which gave rise to the unity of any given organism and its purposes; so was Li. But there the resemblance ceases. The form of the body was the soul; but the great Chinese tradition had no place for souls...Again, Aristotelian form actually conferred substantiality on things, but...the ch'i [material force] was not brought into being by Li, and Li had only logical priority. Ch'i did not depend upon Li in any way. Form was the 'essence' and 'primary substance' of things, but Li was not itself substantial or any form of ch'i... I believe that Li was not in any strict sense metaphysical, as were Platonic ideas and Aristotelian forms, but rather the invisible organizing fields or forces existing at all levels within the natural world. Pure form and pure actuality was God, but in the world of Li and ch'i there was no Chu-Tsai [Director] whatsoever.[18]

More recently, K.O. Thompson emphatically rejected any assumption that "li is in any philosophical sense transcendental or that it occupies a metaphysical realm," as does the concept of Form in Platonic and Aristotelian metaphysics.[19] Thompson insists the principle is not even "logically prior" to material force, in so far as Chu Hsi had no logical framework for even making sense of such a claim. This approach to the understanding of principle, he argues, is "prima facie unacceptable in any case because it presupposes a real separability of *li* and *ch'i*, which Chu Hsi would never countenance."[20] In contrast with the aforementioned "metaphysical" interpretation of *li*, Needham and Thompson insist that *li* denotes the wholly immanent structural composition of material force. For this reason, they prefer to translate *li* as *pattern*, instead of *principle*.

---

[18] Joseph Needham, *Science and Civilization in China* (Cambridge University Press, 1956), volume 2, p. 475.

[19] Kirill Thompson, "*Li* and *Yi* as Immanent: Chu Hsi's Thought in Practical Perspective," *Philosophy East and West* 38, 1 (1988), p. 34.

[20] Ibid., p. 34.

THE THEORY OF LI AND THE NATURAL LAW

How are we to assess the validity of such divergent interpretations of the same concept? In order to answer this question it is important to recognize that this disagreement is not simply about the validity of a Platonic-Aristotelian reading of Chu Hsi's doctrine of principle. This particular problem is merely the symptom of a much deeper dispute that goes to the heart of our understanding of Chinese philosophy as a whole. In terms of this more general debate, the "metaphysical" (Platonic/Aristotelian) interpretation assumes that *li* is to be understood as a kind of *transcendent* principle which is logically and perhaps ontologically independent of the changing material composites of experience. To understand a thing's *li* is to grasp the objective foundation for genuine knowledge which is both descriptive and normative. On this reading, the concept of *li* functions in much the same way as the Platonic theory of Forms or the concept of natural law functions in traditional western philosophical discourse. On the opposing and *organic* view, Chinese philosophy is characterized by the absence of any appeal to transcendent principles or abstract natural laws, according to which nature must conform. *Li* is to be understood, not as a rule imposing order, but more as a pattern *immanent* in the world of change, which is to be evaluated not in terms of its absolute validity, but from the perspective of internal coherence and ongoing praxis.

This problematic is set out most clearly by Needham in his massive *Science and Civilization in China*.[21] In this work, Needham attempts to determine whether there is an understanding of "natural law" or "laws of nature" in the history of Chinese thought analogous to that found in the history of European thought. In this study, Needham distinguishes between "natural law" in the normative (or moral) sense and "laws of nature" in the descriptive (or scientific) sense, i.e., descriptions of regularities operative in nature. Needham insists that historically this distinction emerged out of an originally unified and undifferentiated conception of a universal body of law governing all things. According to Needham, the earliest clear-cut conception of the governance by law of the entire

---

[21] Needham, *Science and Civilization in China*, op.cit. See also Derk Bodde, *Chinese Thought, Society, and Science* (Honolulu: University of Hawaii Press, 1991), pp. 332-355, for a good critical discussion of Needham's analysis.

world, both natural and human, is found in the philosophy of the Stoics. The concept of a universal law applicable to all men and things alike was reinforced by the Judeo-Christian belief in God as the creator and supreme lawgiver. It was systematized by Thomas Aquinas, who distinguished between an eternal law (*lex aeterna*) governing all nonhuman things for all time (which became the basis for the modern scientific concept of "laws of nature") and a natural law (*lex naturalis*) valid for all moral agents (which became the "natural law"). By the seventeenth century the two kinds of law were completely differentiated; with Boyle and Newton, the concept of laws of nature that are "obeyed" by chemical substances and planets alike became commonplace.

Turning to China, Needham finds a very different situation. After subjecting to analysis various terms typically translated as "law" or "rule," Needham concludes that there is no case in which a term has the unambiguous meaning of a "law of nature" or "natural law." Needham's explanation of this conspicuous absence in Chinese thought is attributed to the lack of the idea of a creator god, as supreme celestial lawgiver, and its replacement by a cosmological view of a universe which is uncreated and self-sufficient, operating by means of its own internal forces. Needham refers to this as the "organismic" model of reality. As described by Needham:

> Chinese coordinative thinking...[conceived of]...an extremely and precisely ordered universe, in which things 'fitted, so exactly that you could not insert a hair between them'...But it was a universe in which this organization came about, not because of fiats issued by a supreme creator-lawgiver...It was an ordered harmony of wills without an ordainer; it was like the spontaneous yet ordered in the sense of patterned, movements of dancers in a country dance of figures, none of whom are bound by law to do what they do, nor yet pushed by others coming behind, but cooperate in a voluntary harmony of wills.[22]

---

[22] Needham, *Science and Civilization in China*, p. 286.

> [This]harmonious cooperation of all beings arose, not from the orders of a superior authority external to themselves, but from the fact that they were all part in a hierarchy of wholes forming a cosmic pattern, and what they obeyed were the internal dictates of their own nature.[23]

Needham's "organismic" interpretation of Chinese thought has in one form or another come to dominate recent scholarship, at least among English-speaking writers. Accordingly, Hall and Ames, in their *Thinking Through Confucius* (1987), distinguish between two distinctive ways of understanding the world, which they call the "logical" and the "aesthetic."[24] The logical or rational approach to understanding requires that order be achieved by the application of an antecedent rule or pattern to a given situation. Aesthetic order is achieved by the creation of novel and ever changing patterns of interrelatedness. In particular, "logical order may be realized by the instantiation of principles derived from the Mind of God, or the transcendent laws of nature, or the positive laws of a given society, or from the categorical imperative resident in one's own conscience. Aesthetic order is a consequence of the contribution to a given context of a particular aspect, element, or event which both determines and is determined by the context."[25] Logical thought is characteristic of the western approach to understanding, while aesthetic thought is typically Chinese. Peerenboom parallels the Hall and Ames distinction between logical and aesthetic order with a more epistemological distinction between foundational correspondence and pragmatic coherence theories of knowledge.[26] But whether we focus on ways of knowing or ways of being, the essential point is the same. Chinese thought, which is "organismic," aesthetic, and based on a pragmatic-coherence epistemology, is qualitatively different from the dominant western style of thought, which is hierarchical, logical, and dependent on a foundational correspondence theory of knowledge. As Peerenboom concludes, "the absence of a transcendent

---

[23] Ibid., p. 582.

[24] David Hall and Roger Ames, *Thinking Through Confucius* (Albany: SUNY Press, 1987).

[25] Ibid., p. 16.

[26] R.P. Peerenboom, *Law and Morality in Ancient China*, (Albany: SUNY, 1993), p. 113-118.

source of order becomes the immanence of the Confucian cosmos; heaven, earth, and humans are ontologically all of a piece."[27]

Since the models of interpretation employed by Peerenboom, Hall and Ames are in the spirit of the "organismic" thesis, I will limit my analysis to Needham's characterization. I have no disagreement with Needham's claim that the "organismic" model represents the dominant theme in Chinese thought. There is little doubt that the Neo-Confucian conception of the universe is that of single organism, wherein all things are interrelated in accordance with various patterns of organization. My aim, of course, is not to reevaluate the entire history of Chinese philosophy, but to determine how the philosophy of Neo-Confucianism fits within the dominant conceptual model.[28]

Needham's rejection of the Platonic-Aristotelian interpretation of Chu Hsi's philosophy is based on the claim that *li* is always immanent in nature, never transcendent. *Li* thus represents the *patterns* of organization within the physical universe, not some transcendent principle or law imposed on an otherwise chaotic material force. Needham, like Thompson, stresses the real inseparability of *li* from *ch'i*. In addition, this rejection of *li* as a transcendent law is reinforced by the absence of any supreme lawgiver to be the source of any quasi-legislative world-order.

There are, however, a number of difficulties with this interpretation. While it is true that Chu Hsi stresses the organic unity of *li* and *ch'i* in concrete material things, such that principle is never separated from material force, he repeatedly notes that *li* has *priority* over *ch'i*:

> Fundamentally principle and material force cannot be spoken of as prior or posterior. But if we trace their origin, we are obliged to say that principle is prior. However, principle is not a separate entity. It exists right in material force. Without material force, principle would have nothing to adhere to.[29]

---

[27] Ibid., p. 114.

[28] Bodde, op. cit., p. 344, does acknowledge the existence of a minority position which appears to be congenial to the concept of laws of nature and even a celestial lawgiver along side of and even within the dominant organismic model of reality. Even Peerenboom, who strongly endorses the organismic thesis in general, argues that the recently discovered Huang-Lao text represents a substantial departure from the dominant model. Peerenboom, *Law and Morality in Ancient China*, pp. 75-84.

[29] Chan, *Source Book*, p. 634.

> What are called principle and material force are certainly two different entities. But considered from the standpoint of things, the two entities are one with the other and cannot be separated with each in a different place…[Yet] when considered from the standpoint of principle, before things existed, their principles of being had already existed. Only their principles existed, however, but not as yet the things themselves.[30]

So although principle and material force are co-constituents of material things and thus exist together, Chu Hsi still speaks of the priority of principle over material force. We are told that there must be the principle of a thing before that thing came into existence. As Chu Hsi declares, there is a principle even before there is heaven and earth. But, as noted by Chan, this is not necessarily a question of temporal priority, nor does it require any real separability of principle from material force, as Thompson suggests. Chan correctly concludes that Chu Hsi seems to be arguing that "logically speaking, there must first be the principle before there can be material force which operates according to it, but actually neither can be considered prior to the other [temporally speaking]."[31] In being logically prior, *li* is first in the order of knowing. It is, as we have said, the principle of explanation, and as such can be said to be "transcendent," in the sense that it explains why things are what they are, but not the reverse. Chu Hsi does not require a full-blown logical framework, as Thompson implies, to make sense of this simple epistemological claim.

This transcendent aspect of *li* is acknowledged by Needham himself, who grudgingly concedes that due to the influence of Buddhism, the Neo-Confucians had a tendency "to transcendentalise and supernaturalise the originally naturalistic organicism of Han and pre-Han times," such that the meaning of *li* did acquire "metaphysical overtones" by the time it reached Chu Hsi and "from which he himself was perhaps never quite able to liberate it."[32] Moreover, he concedes that Chu Hsi was unable to discard the belief in at least the slight superiority of *li* as the principle of organization, nor could he "get rid of the idea that a plan implies a plan-

---

[30] Ibid., p. 637.

[31] Chan, *Chu Hsi: Life and Thought*, (Hong Kong: Chinese University Press, 1987), p. 112-113.

[32] Needham, *Science and Civilization in China*, p. 476.

ner who must be prior in time and superior in status to that which is planned."[33]

But should these trace elements of transcendentalism be interpreted as reminiscent of natural law? Again we are faced with the problem created by the apparent absence of a divine lawgiver. Graham, following Needham, suggests that "when we describe what the Neo-Confucians call *li* as 'moral laws' or 'laws of nature', we suggest, however dimly, that they are imposed by a divine legislator on rebellious human nature or on a universe which would otherwise be a chaos."[34] But, notes Graham, for Chu Hsi a principle is a line or pattern that it is natural to follow, not a law which one is bound to obey, "it is also spontaneous, 'thus of itself' (*tzu-jan*), and the idea of a legislator is completely foreign to him."[35] Indeed, that the principles are "made" is expressly denied.

It seems clear that the principles are not made by a supreme lawgiver, in the same way that the laws of nature are conceived of as being commandments issued by God. However, the fact that the principles are not seen as having their source in a divine legislator is not sufficient to warrant the conclusion that they may not be understood as analogous to natural laws. This conclusion begs the question in so far as it assumes that the essence of law is to be in the form of a command willed by some sovereign legislator. While this voluntarist conception of law came to dominate late medieval and modern positivist theories of law, it was expressly rejected by Thomas Aquinas, who favored the intellectualist conception of law. This is why Aquinas defined law, not as a command issued by the will of a sovereign, but as an ordinance of reason.[36] Although what Aquinas calls the *eternal law* is identical with the eternal mind of God, law is understood in purely Platonic terms as the eternal reasons, the rational plan of creation as apprehended by the divine mind. Natural law is nothing more than the rational creature's apprehension of that divine plan in their own nature. Thus to act in harmony with the natural law is simply to act in accordance with the rational principles inherent in one's own nature, which are reflections of the eternal principles in the mind of God.

[33] Ibid., p. 482.
[34] Graham, *Two Chinese Philosophers*, p. 12-13.
[35] Ibid., p.12-13
[36] Thomas Aquinas, *Summa Theologica*, I-II, 90, 1-4.

I suggest that a similar line of reasoning runs through the Neo-Confucian conception of "Heaven" and "the Decree of Heaven." Before the Sung dynasty, the central place in the Confucian cosmology was held by *T'ien* (Heaven), which was conceived as a vaguely personal power controlling nature, in the same way that the Emperor, the "Son of Heaven," controlled the social world. The regular course that all things follow or should follow, from the recurring cycle of the seasons to the customs of human society, is the "Way of Heaven." Put differently, everything which cannot be changed or altered by human manipulation, such as human nature or one's own destiny, is due to the *T'ien-Ming* (Decree of Heaven). The popular association of *T'ien* (Heaven) with *Ti* (God) added a more personal and theistic dimension to the source of the natural and social order, and completed the analogy between Heaven's rule of nature and the emperor's rule of society. Such reasoning in many ways parallels the Thomistic synthesis of Greek rationalism and Judeo-Christian theism, in which the rational principles of Plato and Aristotle are placed in the eternal mind of God. As communicated to humanity, the principles applicable to human conduct became the precepts of natural law. Here the development of Sung Neo-Confucianism takes a different turn, which anticipates the modern secularization of the natural law in the West. The great innovation initiated by the Ch'eng brothers and brought to fruition by Chu Hsi was to raise *li* (principle) to the place formerly held by Heaven, and in so doing to transform heaven and its decrees into different aspects of principle.[37] This might be viewed as the triumph of Chinese *rationalism* over an early mix of rationalism and theism. In this case the absence of a creator-god is filled by a rationalistic conception of principles, which exist "thus of themselves" (*tzu-jan*) and cannot be changed or improved upon by us. To emphasize this absolute or transcendent character, the supreme principle is still called Heaven, and subsidiary principles are called "decrees of heaven". Thus, "what is called heaven is self-dependent (*tzu-lan*) principle."[38] Paraphrasing Mencius, "if it is done without anyone doing it, and happens without anyone causing it, it is [due to] heaven's principle."[39]

---

[37] Graham, *Two Chinese Philosophers*, p. 23.

[38] Ibid., p. 23.

[39] Ibid., p. 23.

This brings us to another parallel in the development of Neo-Confucianism and the natural law tradition, namely the apparent fusion (or confusion) of descriptive and normative statements. Commenting on the thought of Ch'eng Yi, Graham notes that "one reason why Yi-ch'uan is unconscious of any difference between descriptive and normative principles is no doubt that for him what is normative is not so much the assertion of a principle as the definition of a thing."[40] A similar attitude is found among natural law theorists who insist that what a human being ought to do is part of the definition of what it means to be a human being, such that to do what is right is merely to act in accordance with one's rational understanding of human nature. The justification of this attitude must lie in a shared understanding of what it means to define something. Specifically, it must lie in the shared belief that every genuine definition is both descriptive and normative at the same time.

Again Graham can be of assistance here. Graham notes that the Neo-Confucian concept of *li*, in contrast with the Platonic Forms, accounts not for the properties of things, but for "the task it must perform to occupy its place in the natural order."[41] According to Graham, the Neo-Confucians took no interest in the properties of a thing, but focused on the thing's function. If they considered their properties at all, they would have assumed that the properties followed from the thing's function, not the reverse. In effect, to know a thing completely is to know its principle, and to know its principle is to know its function or purpose. Although his aim was to contrast the Platonic-Aristotelian forms with the concept of *li*, Graham has in fact revealed the point of their essential identity. Anyone familiar with the natural law tradition should readily recognize, in this account of Neo-Confucianism, the Aristotelian doctrine of natural teleology. For Aristotle, and later Aquinas, the definition of a thing would include a listing of its essential properties, what Aristotle calls the formal cause or explanation of a thing. But such a definition would be incomplete if it neglected to capture the thing's final cause, i.e., its natural function or purpose. It is this teleological explanation which bridges the gap between a mere description of properties and a conclusion about what a

---

[40] Ibid., p. 29.
[41] Ibid., p. 18.

thing ought to do, for it ought to act in such a way as to fulfill its purpose. Plato approached this sort of explanation with his Form of the Good, Aristotle and Aquinas made teleology part of the description of nature itself, and, if what has been said so far is correct, the Neo-Confucians similarly made the concept of *li* the basis for providing a teleological explanation of reality. This reading of *li* is confirmed by Chu Hsi when he says: "This armchair is an object [literally 'instrument'], that it can be sat in is its principle; the human body is an object, that it speaks and moves is its principle."[42] This is not meant to imply that the Aristotelian "form" and the Neo-Confucian concept of *li* are identical notions, but only that they can be seen to play a similar role in providing a teleological understanding of the nature of things. In so doing, they also provide the basis for a normative ethics grounded in a teleological theory of human nature.

THE THEORY OF LI AND HUMAN NATURE

This brings us back finally to the Neo-Confucian theory of human nature. What role did the concept of *li* play in the defense of the doctrine of the goodness of human nature? In order to answer this question, a brief review of Mencius's discussion of human nature is in order. The general outline of Mencius's doctrine of the goodness of human nature is well known. Human nature is good, thinks Mencius, because human beings are naturally inclined to know and do what is good. This is both an epistemic claim about knowing, i.e., every human being possesses some "innate" understanding of what is morally worthy, as well as a psychological claim about "doing," i.e., every human being is naturally inclined to do what they "know" is right. By learning to act in accordance with this natural inclination, one develops into a fully actualized moral agent. This natural inclination is revealed, for example, in the spontaneous feeling of compassion one has for a young child in danger.[43]

---

[42] Ibid., p. 17.

[43] Hence, in an often quoted passage, Mencius writes: "My reason for saying that no man is devoid of a heart sensitive to the suffering of others is this. Suppose a man were, all of a sudden to see a young child on the verge of falling into a well. He would certainly be moved to compassion, not because he wanted to get in the good graces of the parents, nor because he wished to win the praise of his fellow villagers or friends, nor yet because he disliked the cry of the child." *Mencius*, 2A6.

This clue to understanding of humanity's basic goodness is further elaborated on in the doctrine of the four "beginnings," "germs," or "sprouts" (*duan*). Here we are told that the feeling (heart/mind) of compassion is but one of four innate moral *germs* possessed by every human being:

> The heart of compassion is the germ of benevolence; the heart of shame, of dutifulness; the heart of courtesy and modesty, of observance of the rites; the heart of right and wrong, of wisdom. Man has these four germs just as he has four limbs. For a man possessing these four germs to deny his own potentialities is for him to cripple himself...When these are fully developed, he can take under his protection the whole realm within the Four Seas, but if he fails to develop them, he will not be able to serve his parents.[44]

For Mencius, moral activity is grounded in the four *germs* and their appropriate development. Significantly, human nature is good because it is potentially good. While human nature is equipped with an innate moral sense/inclination to know and do what is right, this moral capacity is inherently weak and fragile. It is in constant need of nurture and cultivation if it is to develop and grow into the appropriate moral virtue.[45]

Mencius's model of human nature and moral virtue is essentially a developmental model within a biological framework. As described by Yearley, "to speak of the nature of something within such a framework is to refer to some innate constitution that manifests itself in patterns of growth and culminates in specifiable forms. These forms display characteristic, regularly repeated kinds of activity, and these activities reveal the normal or natural functioning that represents the excellence of the particular species."[46] The achievement of such excellence, however, depends upon the environment within which the things exists. Like the sowing of barley seeds, to use a Mencian analogy, while the seeds grow, there may

---

[44] *Mencius*, 2A6.

[45] Phillip Ivanhoe notes the importance of the idea of a "germ" or "sprout" as a choice of metaphor to capture these aspects of growth and fragility. Phillip Ivanhoe, *Confucian Moral Self-Cultivation* (New York: Peter Lang Publishing, 1993), p. 27.

[46] Lee Yearley, *Mencius and Aquinas: Theories of Virtue and Conceptions of Courage* (New York: SUNY Press, 1990), p. 58-59.

be some unevenness. This is because "the soil varies in richness and there is no uniformity in the fall of rain and dew and the amount of human effort devoted to tending it."[47] There is no guarantee that a man will become good, in the same way that there is no guarantee that a barley seed will grow and flourish. Nevertheless, what Mencius means by goodness is the presence of these four "sprouts" that can, with effort, grow into the basic human virtues. Thus, "[A]s far as what is genuinely in him is concerned, a man is capable of becoming good...This is what I mean by good. As for his becoming bad, this is not the fault of his native endowment."[48] The major difficulty with this developmental view of human nature is that it reduces human goodness to that of mere potentiality which may never be fully actualized. Such an account, while promising, is practically very similar to any mixed theory of human nature. Both can equally account for the different moral achievements of human agents. In terms of practical effects, i.e., the constant need for moral cultivation and training, there is a relatively thin line between Mencius's optimism and the more pessimistic position advocated by Hsün-tzu. At this level, Mencius's account of the goodness of human nature compares favorably with the natural law account developed by Thomas Aquinas, who similarly grounds our knowledge of the moral precepts of the natural law in the power of human beings to rationally reflect on their own nature. Accordingly, we are able to come to an understanding of certain natural goods by examining a set of natural inclinations, which direct us toward what is good. Since the good has the nature of an end, "it is that all those things to which man has a natural inclination are naturally apprehended by reason as being good, and consequently as objects of pursuit, and their contraries as evil, and objects of avoidance. Therefore, the order of the precepts of the natural law is according to the order of natural inclinations."[49] For example, the natural inclination that all beings have to preserve their life indicates that the preservation of life is a natural good, and the natural desire that all rational beings have to seek the truth and live together with others of their kind indicates that knowledge and social life

---

[47] *Mencius*, 6A7.
[48] *Mencius*, 6A6.
[49] *Summa Theologica*, I-II, 94, 2.

are natural goods. Since these goods are the objects of natural inclinations, we are already predisposed to act in ways consistent with their attainment.

Aquinas, however, goes on to ground the principles of natural law in the eternal law as their ultimate foundation. Since, "the light of natural reason, whereby we discern what is good and what is evil, which is the function of natural law, is nothing else than the imprint on us of the divine light. It is therefore evident that the natural law is nothing else than the rational creature's participation of the eternal law."[50] For Aquinas, the natural law, while discoverable by reflection on human nature is ultimately rooted in the eternal reason of God. This places what is otherwise a simple biological model of morality into a broader metaphysical framework and provides that account of human nature with a deeper ontological foundation.

There are hints of a similar move in the thought of Mencius. We are, for instance, reminded that in developing one's nature one is acting in accordance with Heaven. "For a man to give full realization to his heart is for him to understand his own nature, and a man who knows his own nature will know Heaven. By retaining his heart and nurturing his nature he is serving Heaven."[51] Mencius's quote from the *Book of Odes* reminds one of the traditional natural law context:

> Heaven produces the teeming masses,
> And where there is a thing there is a norm.
> If the people hold on to their constant nature,
> They would be drawn to superior virtue.[52]

Of course, commentators have warned against interpreting these references to Heaven in an unduly "metaphysical" manner. Ivanhoe notes that for Mencius such appeals to Heaven meant only that one should attend to one's natural capacities and by so doing take one's place in the cosmological order.[53] Yearley is even more explicit in denying any greater metaphysical or ontological elements in Mencius's conception of human

---

[50] *Summa Theologica*, I-II, 91, 2.

[51] *Mencius*, 7A1.

[52] *Mencius*, 6A6.

[53] Ivanhoe, *Confucian Moral Self-Cultivation*, p. 27.

nature. "Mencius's employment of a developmental model means that when he declares that human nature is good he refers not to a hidden ontological reality but to the capacities humans possess."[54] Such denials of any recourse to transcendent metaphysical foundations in classical Chinese thought is also in keeping with the naturalistic mode of interpretation favored by many contemporary commentators.

It is my contention, however, that it is just this distinction between a strictly biological/developmental model of human nature and a metaphysical model which lies at the heart of the Neo-Confucian defense of the doctrine of the goodness of human nature. In other words, the Neo-Confucian justification of the Mencian doctrine consisted primarily in supplying a metaphysical foundation for what was otherwise a purely naturalistic account of human nature. Such an account would provide a more coherent explanation of the uniform goodness of human nature, as well as of the fact that not all human beings fully exhibit this constant feature of human nature.

The key to the understanding of the Neo-Confucian justification of the goodness of human nature is the theory of *li*, and the distinction between our "original nature" and our "material nature." Our "original nature" (*pen-hsing*) is *li* itself, human nature in its perfect and pure state logically prior to "material nature" (*ch'i-chih chih-hsing*), which is the composite of *li* and *ch'i*. In contrast with Mencius, original human nature is not identified with our natural tendencies or inclinations as such. Rather, our natural reactions to given external situations are viewed as "indications" of what our "original nature" is really like. Although Chu Hsi portrays himself as merely expounding on the teachings of Mencius, he has in fact provided Mencius's basically psychological account of human nature with a new metaphysical foundation. The "original nature," which is the same in all human beings, is identical with *li*. On the occasions of specific stimuli, the *li* reveals itself and is manifested by a corresponding state of mind. But the state of mind is not the *li* itself, it is merely that which makes the "original nature" known.

In accordance with Chu Hsi's understanding of the Supreme Ultimate, as the totality of *li* present within all things, every human being possesses the same "original nature." This accounts for the original good-

---

[54] Yearley, *Mencius and Aquinas*, p. 60.

ness of human nature. What accounts for the differences between persons and things are their respective endowments of *ch'i*. Since every human being is a combination of *li* and *ch'i*, it is this "material nature," i.e., *li* embedded in *ch'i*, which is the source of their diversity. In contrast with the "prime matter" of the Aristotelian doctrine of hylomorphism, which is a wholly passive capacity to receive form, *ch'i* is an active material force and exists with varying degrees of purity. The purer *ch'i* is more transparent and tends to rise, it is warm and active; while impure *ch'i* is less and tends to sink, it is cool and lethargic. So while all things posses the same *li*, the character of their *ch'i* obscures the *li* within them, permitting only certain *li* to be manifested. It is this which accounts for the diversity among both things and persons.[55]

With this distinction between the "original nature" and the "material nature," Chu Hsi has provided the doctrine of the goodness of human nature with a metaphysical foundation and explained why men behave in ways contrary to what is known to be good. He has also constructed the basis for a theory of moral self-cultivation, which is reminiscent of that found in the natural law tradition. Since the "original nature" is the same as *li*, it is in itself the essence of goodness. "In man, Benevolence, Duty, Manners, and Wisdom (*jen, yi, li, and chih*) are his nature."[56] In virtue of these principles, "man is enabled to have the feelings of commiseration, shame, deference and compliance, and right and wrong."[57] It is only our "material nature" which may obscure and distort our understanding of our genuine nature, and thus prevent us from realizing our true moral selves.[58] The goal of moral self-cultivation is to preserve one's original nature, to return to one's genuine self.

---

[55] See Chan, *Source Book*, p. 620.

[56] Ibid., p. 615.

[57] Ibid., p. 615.

[58] See Chu Hsi and Lu Tsu-ch'ien, *Reflections on Things at Hand* (New York: Columbia University Press, 1967), p. 73.

CONCLUSION

By incorporating the theory of *li* into their understanding of human nature, the Neo-Confucians have in effect replaced the developmental model advanced by Mencius with a "discovery" model of moral self-cultivation.[59] The influence of the Taoist's life in harmony with nature and especially the Chinese Buddhist's pursuit of one's "Buddha-nature" is certainly suggested. The comparison with the natural law tradition is also readily apparent. To return to and preserve one's "original nature" is to act in accordance with the *Tao* (Way) and the Principle of Heaven, since "man's nature is the concrete embodiment of the Way."[60] In so doing, one discovers one's true self. Similarly, for Aquinas, to act in accordance with the natural law is to act in accordance with the eternal law, since human nature is the instantiation of the archetype of human nature in the mind of God. In both cases there is a unity established between the transcendent and the immanent. Moreover, one's understanding of the principles of human nature provides a metaphysical foundation for the pursuit of moral self-cultivation. These principles are independent of one's changeable desires and material circumstances. Thus, to act in accordance with one's "original nature" is to act in harmony with the eternal principles of Heaven found in the very core of one's own unchanging being.

---

[59] See Ivanhoe, *Confucian Moral Self-Cultivation*, for the distinction between the developmental and discovery models of moral self-development.

[60] Chan, *Source Book*, p. 617.

EARLY BUDDHIST INCLUSION OF INTENTIONALITY IN THE LAWS OF CAUSATION[1]

Victor Forte

The soteriological option offered by early Buddhists, as they spread the word of their departed teacher Gautama Buddha throughout Northeast India in the 5th and 4th centuries BCE,[2] was of necessity, presented as a possibility of freedom from transmigration. To know how such freedom could be attained, the natural order of the universe needed to be clearly understood, so that one could find a clear passage beyond nature (i.e. conditioned existence). But most of the work of examining the natural order had already been done before the birth of Gautama. A concern for the functioning of nature had begun in this region centuries earlier within the

---

[1] Although Natural Law theory is a product of Western thought, early Buddhists did share with Natural Law theorists a concern for determining the natural bases for human morality. But the similarities do not extend very much beyond this point. I am interested here in discussing how early Buddhists understood the relation between the natural order and morality, with a particular emphasis on the role that intention plays in this relation, but I will also consider throughout my paper how this understanding can be contrasted with Natural Law theories developed in the West. The first point to be made, as is indicated in the title of this paper, is that the majority of Indian thought during the earliest period of Buddhism (5th-4th centuries BCE), was founded on differing views of causation. Each school of thought developed a teaching on causal law which grounded their ethical systems. Natural law theories by contrast, tend to be based mainly upon observed commonalities of behavior among natural organisms in general, or human beings in particular, and the extent to which certain behaviors are found to be in accord with human reason.

[2] There is some debate over when the historical Buddha died, but most scholars place his birth and death at 563BCE to 483BCE, while others argue that he died about a century later. Another point of clarification is that I have chosen to use the term "early Buddhism" throughout this paper to refer to the Buddhist movement after the death of the historical Buddha. Alternative terminology has been used by others, including, for example "Foundational Buddhism" or "Mainstream Buddhism." It should be kept in mind that in the centuries following Gautama's death a number of different schools of Buddhism did eventually develop, so the term "early Buddhism" does not imply a monolith. Also, the textual evidence used in this paper comes from the Pali Canon. It should be noted that this canon is the only extant collection of early Buddhist texts, and is the product of the only remaining early Buddhist school – *Theravada*. These texts were first written down in Sri Lanka, in the 1st century BCE after about 300–400 years of oral transmission.

Brahmanical clans, resulting in an elaborate system of ritual, performed to harness the powers of the universe, and bring worldly benefits to both priests and patrons. Brahmins called the law of the natural order *Dharma*, literally meaning "to hold up," relating to any activity that supported the cosmos and kept it going. Ritual was itself recognized as *Dharma* since it was understood as integral to the continuation of the natural order. Unless the specialist Brahmanical class consistently performed ritual activities with precision, the natural order would inexorably deteriorate; the world would not be properly held up and, in accordance with *Dharmic* law, everything would fall apart.

Because of the natural world's dependence upon the activities of human beings to maintain natural order, *Dharma* became associated with duty (understood mainly as duty to caste responsibilities). So central is duty to the Hindu understanding of *Dharma*, that the term is most often translated simply as "duty." But in laying the groundwork for understanding and acting in accordance with the natural order through *Dharma*, the Brahmins also uncovered a fundamental human burden—the realization that all human action (*karman*), whether in accordance with *Dharma* or not, was bound up with natural processes. Human beings were trapped within the cycles of nature as they dutifully acted to keep the world from falling apart. If one did not act in accordance with *Dharma* the world would fall apart, and through transmigration, one would fall into lower states of existence. If one acted in accordance with *Dharma*, the natural order would be upheld, but one would still remain within the cycles of nature for innumerable lifetimes of birth and death. Faced with such a dilemma, the problem of human freedom was brought to the level of crisis in Indian consciousness. It was in such a world that early Buddhism was born, and competing with a number of both Brahmanical and heterodox movements, it offered a way out of the bondage that the natural order held over human life.

This paper will consider the implications of the early Buddhist teaching of *intention* (*cetanā*) on the Indian conception of *Dharma*. The topic is useful in a study of eastern views of morality since the teaching is comparatively singular and unique, namely because it claims a relation between the mental state of an agent and the laws of causality. Through this examination it is hoped to clarify first, how early Buddhists understood *Dharma* as a natural moral law, second, how intention was seen as having a causal role in the functioning of the natural order, and third, given this relation between intention and causality, how one could best orient one's life within the natural order.

Contemporary Buddhologists tend to be in agreement that early Buddhists argued that *karma* (Pali: *kamma*) resulted not from action, but from intention (*cetanā*).³ The textual evidence for this position most often comes from the Numbered Discourses (*Anguttara Nikāya*, 6.6.63), which states, "I say monks that *cetanā* is *kamma*; having intended one does a deed by body, word or thought."⁴ This would have distinguished the Buddhist teaching from other movements of the time since it was commonly recognized by the majority of schools that human bondage was inherent in action. In fact, the word *karma* referred to both an action and the results of the action, so for most teachers they were conceptually inseparable. But from the above statement it would seem to mean that for early Buddhists, it is not the action itself, as much as the intention that precedes an action that would determine its *karmic* outcome. Such a position would have been abhorrent to the Jains for example, who maintained that it would necessarily lead to absurd moral consequences, illustrated in the following Jain argument:

> If a savage puts a man on a spit and roasts him, mistaking him for a fragment of the granary; or a baby, mistaking him for a gourd, he will not be guilty of murder! ...If anybody thrusts a spit through a man or a baby, mistaking him for a fragment of the granary, puts him on the fire and roasts him, that will be a meal fit for the Buddhas to breakfast upon...⁵

---

³ For example, Reichenbach has argued that, "Actions performed without intention produce no karma, whereas intention alone is capable of producing it." Williams similarly states, " ...for the Buddha *karman* as an action issuing in appropriate results (necessitating rebirth) ceases to be the external act itself (as it is within e.g. the Brahmanic sacrificial tradition). What are determinitive in terms of 'karmic results' are the wholesome or unwholesome volitions, that is, *intentions*." See Reichenbach, Bruce R, "the law of karma and the principle of causation," *Philosophy East and West*, 38/4 (1988), 399–410, p. 402, and Williams, Paul, with Tribe, Anthony, *Buddhist Thought: A Complete Introduction to the Indian Tradition*, (New York: Routledge, 2000), p. 68.

⁴ See Reichenbach, Bruce R. (1988), p. 402.

⁵ See Kalupahana, David J, *A History of Buddhist Philosophy: Continuities and Discontinuities*, (Honolulu: University of Hawaii Press, 1992), p. 16.

Given the Buddhist teaching of *cetanā* within the climate of prevalent Indian thought on the functioning of *karma*, one might be compelled to consider whether or not the Buddhist view can be defended morally.

However, if we examine a range of the early textual record found in the Pali Canon, the Buddhist position on the relation between intention and *karma* becomes more complex. We can find, for example, numerous instances in these texts where karmic results are explained in terms of action, rather than intention. One of the most repeated explanations of *karma* in the Discourses can be found in the traditional second watch of the Buddha's enlightenment, where, through the power of clairvoyance (known by early Buddhists as the "divine eye") the Buddha was allegedly able to directly cognize how all existences move through the cycles of birth and death according to causal laws. This insight (along with the realization of how to liberate oneself from the cycles of birth and death) is understood by Buddhists as the *Dharma* (Pali: *Dhamma*), in that the Buddha's enlightenment included both the discovery of the laws of the cosmos and how these laws functioned in terms of the bondage of cyclic existence.[6] Gautama was recognized in the tradition as the one who had first realized the *Dharma* and then presented it to the world in the form of his teaching (which is also understood as the *Dharma*).

---

[6] In this understanding of the laws of the cosmos, there is no lawgiver, as we find in Thomist Natural Law Theory. The laws are strictly causal in nature, and are therefore completely impersonal. Early Buddhists did however, recognize the existence of the divine, but there are great differences from Biblical theology. First, there is no creator God according to Buddhism — such a God would be impossible given the universality of the causal interdependence of all phenomena (i.e. a First Cause cannot logically exist). Second, there is not a single God, but many gods existing throughout several different heavenly realms of the cosmos. Third, like human beings, the gods are subject to the bondage of transmigration, as are animals, and so they are therefore not transcendent to nature, but bound to it themselves, although their existences are recognized as being more pleasant than human existence. In this sense, one could argue that Buddhist ethics avoids both the theocentrism (Roman Stoics, Aquinas, Pufendorf) and the anthropocentrism (Grotius, Finnis), upon which Western Natural Law Theory has been constructed. For Aquinas on Natural Law, see Aquinas, Thomas, *Summa Theologica*, Fathers of the English Dominican Province, Trans., Vol. One, Ia-IIae, q. 90–95, (New York: Benzinger Brothers Inc, 1947) p. 993–1017. For John Finnis on Natural Law, see Finnis, John, *Natural Law and Natural Rights*, (Oxford: Clarendon Press, 1980). For a recent study of the history of Natural Law, see Kainz, Howard P., *Natural Law: An Introduction and Re-examination*, (Chicago: Open Court, 2004).

Although the Buddha was the first[7] to have this experience, seeing directly how the *Dharma* functioned, he did not claim a knowledge that was exclusively his own, but taught that others could experience the same insight. So for example, in the Discourse entitled "Fruits of the Homeless Life" ("Sāmaññaphala Sutta"), the Buddha described the process by which any practitioner would evolve towards final liberation, culminating in the 3 watches.[8] The second watch is described as follows:

> And he, with mind concentrated,...applies and directs his mind to the knowledge of the passing-away and the arising of beings. With the divine eye...he sees beings passing away and arising: base and noble, well-favoured and ill-favoured, to happy and unhappy destinations as kamma directs them, and he knows: "These beings, on account of misconduct of body, speech or thought, or disparaging the Noble Ones, have wrong view and will suffer the kammic fate of wrong view. At the breaking-up of the body after death they are reborn in a lower world, a bad destination, a state of suffering, hell. But these beings, on account of good conduct of body, speech or thought, of praising the Noble Ones, have right view and will reap the kammic reward of right view. At the breaking-up of the body after death they are reborn in a good destination, a heavenly world."[9]

---

[7] Actually the tradition does recognize Buddhas who predate Gautama. They are 6 in number and lived in previous ages. It is believed that the Dharma (as law) was discovered by each of these Buddhas, including Gautama, but that the Dharma (as teaching) naturally degrades over time and is eventually forgotten altogether. In due course another man (Buddhas are traditionally always male) discovers the Dharma and the teaching is reintroduced to another age. This means that the Dharma taught by Gautama Buddha will also degrade over time (many believe this deterioration has already been occurring for centuries), and will eventually be forgotten. The next Buddha to come, who will reintroduce the Dharma to the world again is known as *Maitreya*.

[8] It is said in the biographies of the Buddha, after 6 years of searching with various teachers and practices, at the age of 35 he finally sat under a *bodhi* tree (tree of enlightenment) where he vowed to stay until he achieved final liberation. His enlightenment experience occurs over the course of the night which is divided into 3 watches. In the first watch he sees all his past lives (*retrocognition*), in the second watch he sees how all existences move through the cycles of birth and death according to causal laws (*the divine eye*), and in the third watch he realizes the removal of all the corruptions (*āsavas*), sees the causal basis for bondage, and achieves freedom (*nirvāna*).

[9] See *The Long Discourses of the Buddha* (*Dīgha Nikāya*), Maurice Walshe, Trans., (Boston: Wisdom Publications, 1987), p. 107.

There are a number of important elements of the teaching indicated by this explanation of how cyclic existence operates. First, the emphasis here is on conduct or action, and intention is not brought into the equation. Misconduct necessarily leads to bad destinations and good conduct necessarily leads to good destinations. Because conduct (action) has a *necessary* relation to outcome, transmigratory destination is understood to be based upon universal law. Furthermore, this is understood as a natural law rather than a divine one. There is no god in charge to mete out destinations, and so one cannot plead for leniency. One's rebirth is the result of a direct causal determination, based upon *karmic* activity, in accordance with the universal laws (*Dharma*) discovered by the Buddha.

It has been suggested by Potter that *karma* cannot be categorized as a law, but rather as a principle, since one simply chooses to live *as though* there is a karmic result for all conduct, without actually being able to verify that it is so. Laws of nature, like Boyle's law for example, are recognized as such because they are "constantly confirmed and never falsified."[10] Even the Law of Causation, upon which *karma* is based, Potter argues, is a principle rather than a law because causes cannot always be determined, and when this is the case one proceeds on principle by assuming that there must be a cause. This argument however, fails to recognize the claim made in early Buddhism that the functioning of *karma* was fully known first by the Buddha, and then confirmed by a number of others who followed his path. From the standpoint of such knowledge, *karma* functioned not as a principle, but as a universal law, which was verified by all those who acquired this capacity to know. It is from this knowledge that *Dharma*, as law, was discovered. Of course, one may question the possibility of such a knowledge claim, but this is irrelevant to the understanding that the tradition promotes, namely that *karma* functions according to a universal law, which has been discovered by the Buddha and confirmed by the enlightened.[11]

---

[10] See Potter, Karl H, "the naturalistic principle of karma," *Philosophy East and West*, 14/1, (1964), pp. 39–49, p. 39.

[11] This understanding of moral law also contrasts with the majority of Natural Law Theory in that it is not grounded in human reason, but rather, in meditational insight. There is a recognition of the limitations of human reason in early Buddhism for grasping the full import of the ethical teachings. The Buddha argued that relying exclusively on our rational powers would not bring one to awakening since first, some have lesser rational

We also find in the above text that conduct is given three main categories, conduct of body, speech and mind, which can be simply understood as that which one does, that which one says, and that which one thinks. All of these are understood in the canon as actions, including conduct of the mind.[12] It also states in this particular passage that disparaging or praising the Noble Ones has karmic consequences, and we should recognize that this too is understood as action. All these categories of action however, are said to be the result of wrong view, so we should consider what is meant by wrong view in early Buddhist thought. First, this is a very loaded term within the context of its use, since it was argued by early Buddhists that there were many wrong views[13] being offered to the public by other heterodox and Brahmanical schools of thought. "Fruits of the Homeless Life" is a text included in the *Dīgha Nikāya* or *Long*

---

capacities than others, and second, there are times when the use of reason will lead us to erroneous views.

[12] The karmic results of an action that takes place in the mind can be understood in terms of one's consciousness. The more one entertains certain internal thoughts, regardless of their external actions, their consciousness will become conditioned in such a way that these thoughts take on greater and greater mental influence, producing dispositions (*samskāra*) — what we might define as the character of the person. It is also important to note that according to early Buddhists, what continues on after the dissolution of the body is consciousness, known as a *gandhabba*. In order for conception to take place, the mother and the father provide the physical elements (i.e. the gametes), and the *gandhabba* provides the consciousness, or the mental, non-physical elements of the new organism. The *gandhabba* is, in this sense, a carrier of the mental make-up of the previous life from which it derives, including all the mental dispositions (*samskāras*) cultivated through the karmic activities of the organism. Depending on these mental dispositions the *gandhabba* will find itself in one of a number of different cosmological realms, including hells, heavens, animal, human, or other traditionally recognized realms like that of the hungry ghosts (*pretas*) or titans (*asuras*). So the consciousness of any being at the moment of death has a direct causal influence on the conception of new organisms within a natural order that includes realms both seen and unseen by ordinary perception.

[13] In later schools of Indian Buddhist thought, with the emergence of emphasis on *śūnyatā* (*emptiness*), there is the claim that the way of the Buddha means to not hold any view, since all views are conceptually constructed and therefore have no ultimate reality. For example, Nāgārjuna ends his classic collection of verses on the Middle Way, the *Mūlamadhyamakakārikā*, with the verse, "I prostrate to Gautama who through compassion taught the true doctrine, which leads to the relinquishing of all views." See Nagarjuna, *The Fundamental Wisdom of the Middle Way: Nāgārjuna's Mūlamadhyamakakārikā*, Jay L. Garfield, Trans., (New York: Oxford University Press, 1995), p. 83.

Discourses of the Buddha, which was mainly a collection of polemics, aimed against competing schools. In this particular Discourse the Buddha is discussing the merits of the homeless life to King Ajātasattu, the monarch of Magadha, who had committed patricide and was seeking the advice of a number of available teachers on the benefits of the religious life. The text serves both to enumerate the path designed by Gautama Buddha while at the same time, clarifying for the reader why it was superior to all the paths that Ajātasattu had previously explored. In telling Ajātasattu that wrong view leads to lower realms of existence in one's next birth, the Buddha is providing both a moral lesson on how lust for power leads to immoral conduct and subsequent loss of that power in inauspicious rebirths, *and* how following the wrong views of other schools by disparaging the Noble Ones also leads to lower rebirth. Noble Ones are those who live according to *right view* (*sāmma ditthi*) and disseminate its meaning to others through teaching the *Dharma* of the Buddhas. So right view is recognizing the truth of the *Dharma*, and living according to its law, thus living as a Noble One. Even the term "Noble Ones" is contextually polemical since the Brahmanical tradition was founded in Aryan culture. The word Aryan means "Noble One," and it was associated with high caste identity, dominated by priestly and monarchical clans. Therefore, the Buddha is arguing that nobility is a matter of right view and good conduct rather than birth, and subsequent births are also determined by right view and good conduct rather than duty to caste (the Brahmanical meaning of *Dharma*). In describing the functionality of transmigration in this way, early Buddhists are claiming that Dharmic law has been misrepresented by the Brahmanical clans (likewise, by the heterodox teachers), but through the knowledge acquired by the practitioner of the Buddha's path, one will come to know directly for oneself how the causal laws of *karma* and transmigration operate. Only through this knowledge is it then possible to liberate oneself from the bondage that is a function of nature.

So in this explanation of *karma* from the *Dīgha Nikāya* we see there is an emphasis placed on right view. Does this mean that early Buddhists were teaching that right view takes precedence over action in the formation of karma? Again, as we saw in our examination of early Buddhist teachings on the relation between intention and *karma*, we can go to other Discourses where right view is not mentioned in the Buddha's explanation of *karma*. For example, from the *Majjhima Nikāya* (*Middle Length Discourses*), in the "Cūlakammavibhanga Sutta" ("The Shorter Exposition of Action"), a Brahmin student named Subha has asked the Buddha why people are born into inferior or superior lives (why some are sickly or healthy, ugly or beautiful, uninfluential or influential, poor or wealthy, low-born or high-born, stupid or wise). The Buddha provides a detailed account of how different kinds of actions in one's present life will lead to these various kinds of qualities in the next life. He finishes his explanation by stating:

> Beings are owners of their actions, student, heirs of their actions; they originate from their actions, are bound to their actions, have their actions as their refuge. It is action that distinguishes beings as inferior and superior.[14]

Also from the *Majjhima Nikāya*, in the "Sāleyyaka Sutta" ("The Brahmins of Sālā"), the brahmin householders of Sālā ask the Buddha why some beings after death end up in unhappy destinations, even in hell, and why some end up in happy destinations, even in a heavenly world. The Buddha's response begins:

> Householders, it is by reason of conduct not in accordance with the Dhamma, by reason of unrighteous conduct that some beings here, on the dissolution of the body, after death, reappear in states of deprivation, in an unhappy destination, in perdition, even in hell. It is by reason of conduct in accordance with the Dhamma, by reason of righteous conduct that some beings here, on the dissolution of the body, after death, reappear in a happy destination, even in the heavenly world.[15]

In these two examples from the Pali texts we again find no direct mention of intention and only indirect reference to right view in the second verse. So given the differences in the verses from the various Discourses we have discussed so far, is it possible to clarify how the early Buddhists understood the relation between intention, right view and action in the formation of *karma* and the functioning of Dharmic law? In

---

[14] See *The Middle Length Discourses of the Buddha* (*Majjhima Nikāya*), Bhikkhu Ñanamoli & Bhikkhu Bodhi, Trans., (Boston: Wisdom Publications, 1995), p. 1057.

[15] See *The Middle Length Discourses of the Buddha*, (1995), p. 380.

order to do so we can begin by recognizing that the *Buddhadharma*, is understood in terms of causation. The very possibility of determining how a natural system functions is achieved by unraveling the causal patterns that give rise to particular phenomena. *Karma*, as a phenomena determined by the laws of *Dharma* would be no exception. The teachings of early Buddhism are in fact structured as explanations of causal patterns within the phenomenal world, and for this reason the teachings are identified with the law itself and so are also referred to as "*Dharma*."

One might also notice in the early texts that the Buddha is given a number of different titles, one of which is the "*Tathāgata*." This term is quite difficult to translate in a clear and meaningful way and its original meaning is not certain.[16] It denotes both coming and going and is often translated as "thus (*Tathā*) come (*āgata*) and/or gone (*gata*)," signifying that Gautama Buddha is the one who has thus come or gone. The meaning derived from this interpretation is that Gautama has come into the world or gone forth in the world, just as the previous Buddhas had done so, in order to reveal the *Dharma*. That is, the *Tathāgata* is the one who truly knows how causation functions, and reveals to others the way to realizing this knowledge for themselves. He knows how phenomena arise and how they cease due to causal laws, and this is what distinguishes him from other teachers of the period. When the newly acquired disciple Sāriputta reported what he had learned from Gautama Buddha to his friend and fellow skeptic, Mogallāna, he explained the distinctive approach of this teacher by stating, "Whatever be the phenomena that arise from causes, the Tathāgata has expounded their causation as well as their cessation."[17] So the examples taken from the Discourses thus far in our discussion all indicate that the specific reason people were seeking out Gautama Buddha was in order to learn how the laws of causation could reveal the functionality of *karma* and rebirth. As the *Tathāgata*, he was the one who had discovered the causal connections that brought about the results of one's transmigratory journey, and armed with this knowledge, he learned how freedom from rebirth was possible.

---

[16] See Conze, Edward, *Buddhist Thought in India*, (Ann Arbor: The University of Michigan Press, 1962) p. 172n.

[17] See Kalupahana, David J. (1992), p. 21.

So if we want to clarify the relation between *karma*, intention, view, action and rebirth, we would begin by examining how early Buddhists understood their causal relation. First, we have already determined that action is divided into three categories, action of body, speech and mind. All three are given *equal* weight as karmic categories; that is, these three categories of action are not given any relative or hierarchal importance. It is also recognized that all three categories of action produce good or bad kinds of karmic results that lead to either auspicious or inauspicious rebirths. But all actions, whether "righteous" or "unrighteous," are karmic, and they always lead to rebirth. It is recognized that some kinds of rebirth are more pleasing than others, and that orienting one's life towards particular kinds of righteous conduct can bring rewards of more auspicious rebirths, but nevertheless, all rebirth *is* understood as bondage, regardless of its relative quality. Ultimate freedom is only possible by breaking the bonds of rebirth. In the following discourse from the *Samyutta Nikāya* (*Connected Discourses*) for example, the Buddha explains in clear language the early Buddhist understanding of the relation between karma and rebirth.

> And what, bhikkhus is new kamma? Whatever action one does now by body, speech, or mind. This is called new kamma.
>
> And what, bhikkhus, is the cessation of kamma? When one reaches liberation through the cessation of bodily action, verbal action, and mental action, this is called the cessation of kamma.[18]

This text indicates that the Buddha is very much in agreement with the prevalent thought of the day, namely that *karma* is understood as

---

[18] See *The Connected Discourses of the Buddha (Samyutta Nikāya)*, Bhikkhu Bodhi, Trans., (Boston: Wisdom Publications, 2000), p. 1211–1212. We could say that liberation is seen in Buddhism as an ultimate good, and all ethical practices in Buddhism are mainly understood as facilitating its attainment. But liberation itself is not an ethical or virtue-based good, since it is said here to be synonymous with the cessation of action, and ethics is always founded in action. Furthermore, goods fundamental to Natural Law theory, like self preservation or family for example, are actually seen as impediments to liberation for monks and there are strong admonitions by the Buddha against them. A striking example can be found in "The Simile of the Saw" ("Kakacūpama Sutta") *The Middle Length Discourses of the Buddha*, (1995), p. 217–223.

action, and liberation results from the cessation of *karma* through the cessation of action. However, his teaching differs from other systems of thought in three major ways. First, in contrast to the Brahmanical argument, it is not action in relation to the duty of caste that determines rebirth, but rather righteous or unrighteous conduct of body, speech or mind, regardless of caste. Second, in contrast to both materialist schools (*Cārvakas*) and determinist schools (*Ājivikas*), the early Buddhists argued that there *are* karmic repercussions for one's actions, and that Gautama Buddha had in fact, discovered how *karma* truly functioned according to the laws of causation. Third, in contrast to the *Jains*, the Buddha does not recommend an ascetic path based on the elimination of action itself, but rather a path of causal analysis concerned mainly with how agency is related to states of mind and assumptions concerning identity. It is because of this inclusion of mental phenomena in the functionality of karmic causality that the relation between right view, intention and action must be examined.

What we have established thus far is that early Buddhists, like most other Indian schools of the time, did identify *karma* with action (not intention) and that they also recognized that *karma* always brought about rebirth. Once an action is performed, whether through body, speech or mind, karmic results are a necessary effect. In order to undo the effects of *karma* one must therefore determine what it is that produces any action. If we know what the cause of an action is, then by eliminating that cause both action and the results of action would be eliminated. As the *Tathāgata*, the Buddha's attainment of freedom is understood to have resulted from his discovery of the laws of causation. We find that the basic application of this discovery in Buddhist thought is to recognize first, that for any phenomena to arise, it must have a cause, and in order to eliminate this phenomena we can do so by eliminating the cause. Second, if we want to bring about the phenomena, we do so by bringing about the cause, and then the phenomena will naturally arise. This understanding of causation is presented in early Buddhism as *dependent origination (paticcasamuppāda)*, and is expressed by the Buddha throughout the Discourses in the following formula:

> When this exists, that comes to be; with the arising of this, that arises. When this does not exist, that does not come to be; with the cessation of this, that ceases.[19]

So essential to the path of the early Buddhists is this tenet on the law of causation, that the Buddha is said to have declared, "One who sees dependent origination sees the Dhamma; one who sees the Dhamma sees dependent origination."[20]

Seeing the *Dhamma* is having right view, and having right view is recognizing the law of causation in one's own day to day life. In being conscious of the functionality of causation, one can develop a greater awareness of how certain causes bring about certain effects, either beneficial or detrimental to both one's present life and one's rebirth. The majority of Buddhist practices are based upon this fundamental notion. One practices the path by cultivating the causes that bring about wholesome or beneficial karmic results, and eliminating the causes that bring detrimental karmic results. We have already seen that these karmic results are due to either righteous or unrighteous actions, so the main question is then, what are the causes of these two kinds of action? The Buddha is said to have found that unrighteous actions are based in the three unwholesome roots (*tiakusala-mūlāni*), defined as ignorance, anger and greed. The three unwholesome roots are associated with a number of "defilements" (*kleśas*, Pali: *kilesas*), further delineating the possible unwholesome states of mind.[21] Righteous actions are based in the opposites of the unwholesome roots, in the wholesome states of mind, namely wisdom (*prajñā*), loving-kindness (*mettā*) and compassion (*karunā*). By cultivating wisdom, ignorance can be eliminated, by cultivating loving-kindness, anger can be eliminated and by cultivating compassion, greed can be eliminated.[22] Therefore, the causal chain, as we understand it thus far, for

---

[19] See *The Middle Length Discourses of the Buddha* (1995), p. 927.

[20] See *The Middle Length Discourses of the Buddha*, (1995), p. 283.

[21] The *Kleśas* include among others, ill will, revenge, contempt, envy, avarice and deceit. See *The Middle Length Discourses of the Buddha*, (1995), p. 372, for the Buddha's discussion on the relation between the *Kleśas* and "unhappy destinations."

[22] This cultivation is achieved through a large, systematic array of disciplines designed to purify the mind for the attainment of liberation. The main ones however, are: (1) The practice of the precepts (not killing, not stealing, not lying, not engaging in sexual misconduct, not using intoxicants), (2) The practice of the Noble Eight-fold Path (right view,

bringing about inauspicious rebirths looks like the following:

Kleśas —›Unrighteous Action (*Karma*)—›Inauspicious Rebirth.

In order to bring about an auspicious rebirth, the unwholesome roots must be replaced by wisdom, loving-kindness and compassion, which will lead to righteous actions, the cause of good karmic results and auspicious rebirths. This understanding is based on the early Buddhist formula of dependent origination. To the extent that the *kleśas* are present, unrighteous action will arise, and to the extent the *kleśas* cease by replacing them with wholesome states of mind, righteous actions will arise.

Notice here that both the *kleśas* and their replacements are not themselves actions, but are mental states of greed, anger, ignorance or wisdom, loving-kindness and compassion. For example, loving-kindness does not mean doing kind deeds, but is the mental state that gives rise to kind deeds. The early Buddhists recognized then that causation, in terms of human action, is dependent upon the mental state of the agent which precedes the action. Therefore, the effects of human action on the natural order are founded first, not in the action, but in the mental state that gave rise to the action, for the action is dependent on the mental state, and will arise only if the mental state upon which it is dependent is present. From a practical standpoint this means the early Buddhists realized that in order for one to change one's conduct, it is most advantageous to begin by first changing one's mind, then changes in conduct will follow naturally through causal necessity.

If this is the case, then the intention of the agent must also be recognized in the causal chain that gives rise to either righteous or unrighteous actions. We have just established that there is a dependency inherent in action upon the mental state that precedes it, and if we look for the mental state which most immediately precedes an action, we could define this

---

right volition, right speech, right action, right livelihood, right effort, right mindfulness, right concentration), and (3) The practice of various forms of meditation. Meditation has three main forms: (1) Practices to still the mind, like mindfulness of breathing, followed by (2) *Vipassanā*, or insight meditation, employed to analyze the true nature of phenomena, which all exhibit the three characteristics of unsatisfactoriness (*dukkha*), impermanence (*anicca*), and non-self (*anatta*, Sanskrit: *anātman*), and (3) Meditation to bring about wholesome states of mind like *mettabhavana*, the meditation on loving-kindness.

mental state as "intention."[23] In order for one to act, one can only bring about the action by first intending to act. It would also mean that intention is related to the *kleśas* in that unwholesome, or defiled states of mind, will give rise to unwholesome intentions. So to further refine our understanding of the causation that leads to an inauspicious rebirth we would place "Intention" between "*kleśa*" and "Unrighteous Action," giving us the following causal chain:

Kleśas —› Intention—›Unrighteous Action *(Karma)*—›Inauspicious Rebirth

For example, if one's mind is defiled by deceit (*kleśas*), this will give rise to the intention to do deceitful things, necessarily leading to deceitful actions, bad karma, and an inauspicious rebirth. This explanation is also in agreement with the original statement we cited from the *Anguttara Nikāya*, "I say monks that *cetanā* is *kamma*; having intended one does a deed by body, word or thought." In this statement the Buddha does say in fact that intention *is* karma ("*cetanā* is *kamma*"), but this is the case only because intention leads *necessarily* to action – "having intended one does a deed by body, word or thought." So the early Buddhists are not relating intention to *karma* independent of action, but only because intention is understood as necessarily leading to action. If this is recognized as the case, then one can eliminate certain kinds of action by the practical approach of eliminating the intention that gives rise to the action, accomplished through the cultivation of particular states of mind. This would

---

[23] It is important here to distinguish what we have already discussed as karmic mental actions (i.e. actions of the mind), and what we are referring to as mental states and intentions. We could begin by stating that the mental states are internal conditioning forces or *samskāras*, of which the *kleśas* are one type. They bring about particular activities of the mind. Mental action is therefore understood as conscious mental activity that is dependent upon what are largely unconscious mental conditioning forces, and these conditioning forces are associated with the entire transmigratory history of an organism. However, there is a somewhat circular interdependence between them in that one also conditions the mind by thinking particular thoughts, even for example, as a part of meditational practices in order to give rise to particular wholesome dispositions. These dispositions in turn further condition the mind to think certain kinds of thoughts. So then the dispositions (*samskāras*) give rise to intention (*cetāna*) which then give rise to thoughts (mental actions). In this sense karmic formations are neither deterministic (one can train one self to have certain dispositions through thinking certain kinds of thoughts) nor are they a matter of complete free will (we are conditioned to think in certain ways).

also mean that the cessation of all intention would lead necessarily to the cessation of all action. As was stated earlier from the Discourses, liberation means the cessation of action. But unlike the Jains, the early Buddhists taught that the cessation of action could not be achieved by attempting to eliminate action itself, but by eliminating the intentions upon which all actions are dependent.

So to argue the early Buddhists were teaching that it is intention, rather than action which produces karmic effects, is misleading, and takes the statement from the *Anguttara Nikāya* out of context. If we include this statement within the larger corpus of Pali texts we find that it only confirms the priority given to action in the meaning of *karma*. It is more accurate to say that the emphasis placed on the relation between intention and *karma* serves to promote an awareness of the chain of causation that brings about particular actions, and allows for the practical application of mental cultivation, aimed at the elimination of specific detrimental forms of *karma*, eventually leading to the liberation that is the end of *all* forms of *karma*.

If we understand the teaching in such a manner, then the moral consequences described earlier from the cited Jain text are no longer problematic, since we find in its logic the same kind of misrepresentation of the Buddhist position as we do in contemporary, Western Buddhology. There is an assumption that the Buddhist teaching means action has no karmic consequence, and only intention matters in determining karmic outcomes. Used as a polemic against the Buddhists, the example given of a person (savage or not) mistaking a man for a fragment of the granary, or a baby for a gourd, is of course absurd, but serves as a shocking illustration to drive home the moral collapse that results from asserting that *karma* is a matter of intention, rather than action. We can also imagine in ordinary circumstances, that a person might intend to do something good, yet their actions may lead to bad results, or they may intend to do something bad, but their actions somehow lead to results that are good on some level. This is one of a number of common moral dilemmas human beings face when observing how justice, or lack of justice, seems to function in the world around them. These observed inconsistencies in the functioning of justice often lead to questions concerning the moral order of the universe, whether that order is understood to be divinity-based,[24] or *karma*-based.[25]

Early Buddhism does attempt to present an understanding of the natural order that is fundamentally moral. The causal laws discovered by the Buddha (i.e. *Dharma*) are said to function in a necessary, moral pattern. As we have seen in the Discourses thus far, the causal laws of *karma* and rebirth are presented with a certainty that moral actions will give rise to a more pleasant existence, both in present and future lives, while immoral actions will give rise to more unpleasant existences. But the early Buddhists also faced the difficulties of explaining how intention and *karma* would function causally in various kinds of possible cases. For example, in the *Milindapañha*, or the *Questions of Milinda*, the Buddhist teacher Nāgasena is asked a number of probing questions from King Milinda concerning the ways in which *karma* operates in various human situations. The king is mainly concerned with how to go about avoiding karmic demerit, while building up stores of merit, which would provide auspicious future rebirths. When asked about the karmic results of committing evil acts *unknowingly*, Nāgasena responds that an evil act committed unknowingly brings *high* stores of *demerit*. In McDermott's examination of the text, he argues that this response by Nāgasena contradicts the canonical position concerning intention and karma.

> ...we must conclude that Nāgasena's position is really quite different from the usual canonical position. Nāgasena holds that serious demerit accrues to anyone who takes the life of another, even when this is done without awareness and, hence, by implication, unintentionally. Nāgasena, then, here appears to represent the view that the actual physical act is of greater

---

[24] The main moral questions concerning divinity-based understanding of the universe center on the *theodicy problem*, or the problem of divine justice. The theodicy problem can be expressed in terms of three main premises: (1) An omnipotent God exists, (2) This God is benevolent, (3) There is suffering in the world. If both (1) and (2) are held to be so, how can (3) be reasonably explained?

[25] For recent critical examinations of *karma*-based systems of morality see Kaufman, Whitley R. P, "karma, rebirth, and the problem of evil," *Philosophy East and West*, 55/1 (2005), p. 15–32, and Wright, Dale, "critical questions towards a naturalized concept of karma in Buddhism," *Journal of Buddhist Ethics*, 11 (2004), p. 78–93.

ethical significance than is the thought, motive, or intention behind it. In this he has moved away from the distinctively Theravāda Buddhist notion....we have here an indication that the definition of *kamma* as *cetanā* and what follows upon it was maintained within Buddhism at times with difficulty; for Nāgasena...did not believe in the universal desirability of maintaining the unwavering stress on '*cetanā*' in this definition.[26]

If we maintain however, that the canonical position *does* agree that "the actual physical act is of greater ethical significance than is the thought, motive or intention behind it," then there is no contradiction to be found in Nāgasena's response to King Milinda. His response only confirms and supports the canonical position.

Nevertheless, in the case discussed by Nāgasena, the agent's state of mind is still of great significance. If one commits a wrongful act unknowingly, then it is the lack of awareness that brought about the possibility of the wrongful act. Even though the karmic demerit derives directly from the action, the action is still dependent upon the level of intention. If one acts unknowingly, then the level of intention is low, but this is still indicative of a state of mind that was causally connected to the act. Furthermore, we should not assume that acting unknowingly is somehow equivalent to being liberated due to intention being absent in both cases. The difference is that the liberated knowingly act without intention, (thus not acting in the ordinary sense, and so without *karma*), while in this example, we have the case of someone unknowingly acting without intention (and so bound to *karma*). Nāgasena's answer therefore neither misinterprets the canon by prioritizing intention over action in the formation of *karma*, nor does it negate the importance of the state of mind of the agent in question.

---

[26] See McDermott, James P, "kamma in the Milindapañha," *Journal of the American Oriental Society*, 97/4, (1977), p. 460–468.

THE THIRD WAVE? THE GENERATION THEORY OF HUMAN RIGHTS
Eric Engle

INTRODUCTION

Aristotle describes humans as rational talking animals living in a society organized to obtain not merely the means of life but also "the good life," a fact true in all times and places.

Consequently, there is nothing uniquely "western" about human rights. [1] Human rights are universal as an expression of rationality, as aspirational goals of societies seeking to secure the good life for their members and as a manifestation of natural law. However, human rights are not inevitable. They are only a possible and not a necessary consequence of economic development. Histories of human rights usually propose that the concept has evolved through at least three separate historical waves. This historical account is only roughly accurate. Human rights are a key aspect of the transformation of the international system from a hierarchical centralized state model to a decentralized network of state and non-state actors.

A. THE PARADIGM SHIFT: FROM SOVEREIGN STATES TO INDIVIDUAL RIGHTS[2]

The Westphalian system regarded only states as subjects of international law enjoying absolute and inviolable power within their own borders. [3] This system has been transformed: state power is constrained by the rights of non-state actors' rights under international law against state

---

[1] By western I mean the Americas and Europe. By southern I mean Africa, South Asia and South America. By Asian I mean all of Asia excepting Russia. By Northern I mean North America, Europe and Japan.

[2] The "shift in sovereignty accompanying globalization has meant that non-state actors are more involved than ever in issues relating to human rights."Dinah Shelton, "Protecting Human Rights In A Globalized World," 25 *B.C. Int'l. Comp. L.Rev.* 273, 273 (2002) *available at:* http://www.bc.edu/bc_org/avp/law/lwsch/journals/bciclr/25_2/06_TXT.htm.

[3] Individuals and non-state actors in the Westphalian system were considered mere "objects" of international law. Antonio Cassese, *Human Rights in a Changing World*, Polity Press *at* 14 (1990).

and private actors.[4] As a result[5] of the second world war[6]—the second failure of the Westphalian system to maintain global peace in as many generations—individuals and organizations were tried for crimes under international law[7] crimes against peace, crimes against humanity,[8] and war crimes[9] at the Nürnberg tribunals.[10] The defences raised by the accused—sovereign immunity, official immunity,[11] *nul crimen sine lege,*[12] *respondeat superior*,[13] compulsion,[14] and of one's duty to obey[15] the orders of a lawfully appointed superior[16]—were all rejected. Suddenly states' rights were qualified by individual's duties.

Knowingly or not, in assigning a legal duty to individuals to obey cer-

---

[4] International Human Rights law assigns rights and even duties to individuals. Theodor Meron, *Human Rights and Humanitarian Norms as Customary Law* (Oxford: Clarendon, 1989) at 101, and protects individuals against state action and even against private action (Theodor Meron, id.at 98).

[5] Louis B. Sohn, "The New International Law: Protection Of The Rights Of Individuals Rather Than States*,"* 32 Am. U. L. Rev. 1, 1 (1982).

[6] Antonio Cassese, *supra* note 2 at 15 (arguing that the second world war inaugurated a radical reconceptualization of international law).

[7] Robert D. Sloane, *supra* note 15 at 144. (Human rights documents founded sprang from the ruins of the Second World War).

[8] For a discussion of contemporary issues in crimes against humanity *see*: Simon Chesterman*, An Altogether Different Order: Defining The Elements Of Crimes Against Humanity* 10 Duke J. of Comp. & Int'l L. 307 (2000) *available at:*http://www.law.duke.edu/shell/cite.pl?10+Duke+J.+Comp.+&+Int'l+L.+307

[9] Louis B. Sohn, *supra* note 5 at 11.

[10] Charter Of The International Military Tribunal August 8, 1945, Article 6, *available at* http://www.yale.edu/lawweb/avalon/imt/proc/imtconst.htm.

[11] IMT Art. 7.

[12] Paul Feuerbach Lehrbuch des gemeinen in Deutschland gueltigen peinlichen Rechts (1st ed. 1801) cited in: The Trial of Adolf Eichmann, Defence Submission 2 available at: http://www.nizkor.org/hweb/people/e/eichmann-adolf/transcripts/Sessions/Defence-Submission-02-01.html.

[13] Jeanne L. Bakker, *The Defense Of Obedience To Superior Orders: The Mens Rea Requirement*, 17 Am. J. Crim. L. 55, 57 (1989).

[14] Id. Jeanne L. Bakker, *The Defense Of Obedience To Superior Orders: The Mens Rea Requirement*, 17 Am. J. Crim. L. 55, 62 (1989).

[15] *Id.* at 58.

[16] IMT Art. 8. This is perhaps the most counterintuitive problem posed by the Nuremberg principles: the duty of an individual to disobey the sovereign under interna-

tain norms *erga omnes*[17]—to *disobey*, under certain circumstances, the command of the sovereign—the International Military Tribunal broke from the Westphalian model. The tribunal was forced to recognize universal principles of natural justice.[18] The non-retroactivity of law (no *ex post facto* criminal laws) was a principle of law since at least the French *Déclaration des Droits de l'Homme* (Art. 8)—Hobbes mentions the principle even earlier.[19] These breaches of the principle of legality—that crime would be defined only prior to its commission—and the Westphalian principle of the absolute nature of sovereignty could only be justified *via* a theory of natural law:[20] the war crimes were such a basic and self evident violation of the inherent dignity of humans that they were implicitly prohibited under *ius* naturale.[21] To escape accusations of vio-

---

tional law is incongruent with the rationale of the Westphalian system. Once a duty was imposed on individuals to disobey the orders of the sovereign, the argument that only the sovereign should be the intermediary of the individual in the international arena becomes illogical. How can one be required at once to disobey the sovereign and be expected to rely on that sovereign for protection internationally? By implication Nuremberg ended the monopoly of the state as representative of the individual internationally.

[17] Alfred P. Ruben, "Actio Popularis, Jus Cogens, and Offenses Erga Omnes," 35 N. Eng. Law Rev. 265, 267 (2001) available at: http://www.nesl.edu/lawrev/Vol35/35-2/rubin.pdf.

[18] Nuremberg Trial Proceedings Volume 19, One Hundred And Eighty-Seventh Day, Friday, 26 July 1946 available at: http://www.yale.edu/lawweb/avalon/imt/proc/07-26-46.htm.

[19] Hobbes, *Leviathan* (1651), Chapters 27-28.

[20] "Lex mala, lex nulla"—an evil law is no law at all. Thomas Aquinas, Summa Theologica, (2d Ed., 1920 citing Augustine "that which is not just seems to be no law at all" (De Lib. Arb. i, 5) available at: http://www.newadvent.org/summa/209502.htm.

[21] For example, when Eichmann was tried for "crimes against the Jewish people", the trial court's judgement (not necessarily the appeal!) relies on Blackstone arguing that mala in se can be prohibited ex post-because they are violations of natural law but also attempts to make a questionable distinction between ex post facto and retroactive laws. In contrast the Appellate judgment relies on the positivist Kelsen: "There is no rule of general customary international law forbidding the enactment of norms with retrospective force, so called ex post facto law" (Kelsen, Peace through Law (1944) p. 87) and Stone "There is clearly no principle of international law embodying the maxim against retroactivity of criminal law" (Julius Stone, Legal Controls of International Conflict (1959) p. 369). The court even points out: "...it is hardly necessary to invoke natural law to condemn the mass slaughter of helpless human beings. Murder is generally taken to be a crime in positive international law." Friedmann (Legal Theory, 4th ed., p. 316). Despite these positivist references the Israeli supreme court still felt compelled to contradict its positivism and rely,

lating the principle *nullum crimen, nulla poena, sine praevia lege*[22] the court had to acknowledge arguments based on a theory of universal law—natural justice.

Thus, the courts at Nuremberg and in *Eichmann* could not escape from the idea of morality despite the fact that the entire tendency of legal theory since at least 1880 was toward positivism, which dismissed theories of natural law as pre-scientific, wishful thinking or naive. Indeed, much immoral conduct is not sanctioned by law. This split between law and morality can be reconciled if we recognize that law is about force and justice is about morality. Positivism and natural law can in fact be linked (as Hobbes and Aristotle do)[23] by distinguishing natural *law* (lex naturalis)[24] from natural *justice* (Cicero,[25] Aquinas,[26] and many others). That resolves the supposed dichotomy between positivism and natural law.[27]

Nuremberg broke from the Westphalian model, resurrected naturalism but was problematic because the victorious powers had also committed war crimes: mass aerial bombardment of civilian populations,[28] use of chemical weapons (specifically, white phosphorous) and even atomic

---

finally, on: "universal moral values and humanitarian principles which are at the root of the systems of criminal law adopted by civilised nations". Israel v. Eichmann, Criminal Case No. 40/61 (district court) available at: http://www.nizkor.org/hweb/people/e/eichmann-adolf/transcripts/Judgment/Judgment-001.html; Israel v. Eichmann (S. Ct.) available at: http://www.nizkor.org/hweb/people/e/eichmann-adolf/transcripts/Appeal/Appeal-Session-07-01.html.

[22] James Popple, The right to protection from retroactive criminal law, 13 Crim. L. Jnl. 4, 251-62 (1989); 2 Australasian Law Students' Association Journal, 5-18 (1989) available at: http://cs.anu.edu.au/~James.Popple/publications/articles/retroactive/2.shtml.

[23] Aristotle, *Politics*, Book V.

[24] Hobbes, Leviathan, Ch. XIV, para. 3. Hobbes' lex naturalis is the law of self preservation, implicitly via the use of force if necessary.

[25] Cicero, *The Republic* at *III, XXII* (Loeb Classical Library, 1950) *Available at:* http://www.thelatinlibrary.com/cicero/repub.shtml (lat.).

[26] Thomas Aquinas, Summa Theologica, Secunda Secundae Partis §57 (Right) available at: http://www.newadvent.org/summa/3.htm.

[27] See, Eric Engle, Critical Legal Studies in America, *at:* http://www.gradnet.de/alt/pomo2.archives/pomo2.papers/engle00.htm (2000)

[28] The League of Nations had already condemned aerial bombardment of civilians: Protection Of Civilian Populations Against Bombing From The Air In Case Of War, Unanimous resolution of the League of Nations Assembly, September 30, 1938.

Engle 81

bombardment.29 The shadow of Nuremberg points an accusing finger at those who judged but were not judged.30 After Nuremberg the international legal system changed radically: states would no longer have a right to launch wars of aggression and could only resort to force in self defence.31 An international governing body, the United Nations, with the power to approve or disapprove of the use of force,32 arose like a Phoenix out of the ashes of the failed league of nations and devastated continents.

Ultimately the post-war system outlawed wars of aggression,33 recognized a right to humanitarian assistance34 and a right of humanitarian intervention,35 individual and corporate liability in crime or in tort under

---

Available at: http://lessons.ctaponline.org/~murphy_s/Nuclear/Text%20Evidence/international_law_on_the_bombing.htm.

29 The use or threat to use nuclear weapons is probably a war crime and/or a crime against humanity. *See: On the Legality of the Threat or Use of Nuclear Weapons*, International Court of Justice, The Hague, 8 July 1996; Resolution On Nuclear Weapons United Nations, November 24, 1961, General Assembly Resolution 1653.

30 See, e.g., Alfred P. Rubin, *Actio Popularis, Jus Cogens And Offenses Erga Omnes?*, 35 New Eng. L. Rev. 265, 267, 280 (2001). "no such tribunal existed outside of various victors' tribunals (like the post-WWII allied tribunals at Nuremberg, Tokyo and elsewhere), which did not apply the same 'law' to the victors' leaders that they applied to the leaders of the vanquished state or forces."

31 "Article 2(4) of the UN Charter comprehensively prohibits the use of force, thereby surpassing the 1928 Kellogg-Briand Pact's prohibition of going to war as a political means." Jost Delbruck, *A More Effective International Law Or A New "World Law"?— Some Aspects Of The Development Of International Law In A Changing International System*, 68 Ind. L.J. 705, 707-708 (1993).

32 Charter of the United Nations, Ch. VII, Art. 41 available at: http://www.un.org/aboutun/charter/.

33 Jost Delbruck argues that in the post-cold war era the definition of "aggression" is becoming broader. *See:* Jost Delbruck, *supra* note 32 at 708.

34 Humanitarian assistance appears undefined in international law. For attempts at definitions see, Noëlle Quénivet, Humanitarian assistance: a right or a policy?, The Journal of Humanitarian Assistance (June, 2000) at: http://www.jha.ac/articles/a030.htm and also, Songiee Song, NGOs and UN System in Humanitarian Assistance in War Zones: Focusing on Somalia and Rwanda, (M.A. thesis, 2000) at: http://gias.snu.ac.kr/i/i-thesis/i-0008thesis/sisong.pdf. In U.S. domestic law humanitarian assistance is defined at 22 U.S.C. § 2296 (b)(2) as "assistance to meet humanitarian needs, including needs for food, medicine, medical supplies and equipment, education, and clothing." available at:

http://caselaw.lp.findlaw.com/casecode/uscodes/22/chapters/32/subchapters/i/parts/xii/sections/section_2296.html.

35 "Humanitarian intervention is the threat or use of force by a state, group of states, or

international human rights law and accorded rights and duties to non-state actors including non-governmental organizations (NGOs),[36] guaranteeing human rights in international declarations, resolutions, and conventions. At the same time universal[37] jurisdiction expanded.[38] State power simultaneously 1) devolved "downward" to regional, provincial, and municipal entities 2) transferred "upward" to *supra*-national economic and political organizations, and 3) privatized "outward" to corporations and individuals. All of these changes have imposed real limits on the formerly absolute sovereign power of "The State".

1. Elaboration of Global Human Rights Norms: Opinio Juris

A key feature of the post-Westphalian world is the rise of a global conventional system of universal norms, with regional or global jurisdiction aiming at universal membership alongside similar hemispheric and Continental conventions.[39] These conventions are promulgated by inter-

---

international organization primarily for the purpose of protecting the nationals of the target state from widespread deprivations of internationally recognized human rights." Tania Voon, *Closing The Gap Between Legitimacy And Legality Of Humanitarian Intervention: Lessons From East Timor And Kosovo*, 7 UCLA J. Int'l L. & Foreign Aff. 31, 34 (2002) There are some historical precedents even prior to the world wars for the right of humanitarian intervention in order to protect human rights. *See:* Louis B. Sohn, *supra* note 5 at 5.

36 The extent of NGO's appears to be growing, and NGOs are even implicated in the question of whether states have a right of intervention to provide humanitarian assistance. See C. Stahn, *NGO's and Internationational Peacekeeping* 61 ZaÖRV 379 (2003).

37 William C. Plouffe, *Sovereignty In The "New World Order": The Once And Future Position Of The United States, A Merlinesque Task Of Quasi-Legal Definition,* 4 Tulsa J. Comp. & Int'l L. 49, 54 (1996). (Recognizes at least five bases for jurisdiction under international law "(1) the territorial principle, (2) the nationality principle, (3) the protective principle, (4) the passive personality principle, and (5) the universality principle.").

38 But *see:* D. Bowett, *Jurisdiction: Changing Patterns of Authority over Activities and Resources* in R. Macdonald, D. Johnston (eds.) *The Structure and Process of International Law: Essays in Legal Philosophy Doctrine and Theory* (Martinus Nijhof, 1986). Acknowledges the existence of universal jurisdiction under the passive and active personality principle and the protective principle (560-562), but argues that while universal jurisdiction exists in cases of piracy and air piracy, that (despite *Eichmann* and the 1949 Geneva Conventions!) universal jurisdiction does not or should not exist as to war crimes, terrorism, or apartheid (563-564).

39 For „conventional," see Human Rights in a Changing World, Antonio Cassese supra note 2 at 22; for "system," see Philip Alston, Final report on enhancing the long-term

national organizations and try to protect human rights and to guarantee freedom of commerce. Liberal economic theory postulates that free trade increases prosperity and reduces the likelihood of war by de-linking economy and territory. "[T]hree-quarters or more of United Nations member states have ratified five of the six human rights treaties."[40] These networks of norms have been constantly expanding and are interlocking, i.e. they are mutually reinforcing.[41]

The various human rights treaties usually feature enforcement mechanisms that include at least an expert monitoring body with power to hear petitions from state parties and sometimes even from individuals[42] or

---

effectiveness of the United Nations human rights treaty system (Geneva : UN, 1997); for "norms," see Henry J. Steiner & Philip Alston, International Human Rights in Context: Law, Politics, Morals (2d ed. 2000) at 69,136; for "regional," see Jose E. Alvarez, "The New Treaty Makers," 25 B.C. Int'l & Comp. L. Rev. 213 to 25 B.C. Int'l & Comp. L. Rev. 213, 217-218 (2002) (nearly half of all multilateral treaties developed by the U.N.); for "global," see Elsa Stamatopoulou, "The Development Of United Nations Mechanisms For The Protection And Promotion Of Human Rights," 55 Wash. & Lee L. Rev. 687 to 55 Wash. & Lee L. Rev. 687, 688-689 (1998) (describes the global UN convention system— CEDAW, CAT, ICCPR, CESCR, and CERD); for "membership," see Jose E. Alvarez, supra at 220 (describes formative processes of multilateral treaties); for "hemispheric," see, for example, the [Inter] American Convention on Human Rights, O.A.S. Treaty Series No. 36, 1144 U.N.T.S. 123 entered into force July 18, 1978 available at: http://heiwww.unige.ch/humanrts/oasinstr/zoas3con.htm; for "Continental," see [European] Convention For The Protection Of Human Rights And Fundamental Freedoms, 213, available at: http://heiwww.unige.ch/humanrts/instree/z17euroco.html; and for "conventions," see Jose E. Alvarez, "The New Treaty Makers," 25 B.C. Int'l & Comp. L. Rev. 213 to 25 B.C. Int'l & Comp. L. Rev. 213, 216-217 (2002) (notes proliferation in treaties and that the proliferation of treaties is accompanied by the rise in international organizations).

[40] Caroline Dommen, *The U.N. Human Rights Regime: Is It Effective?* 91 Am. Soc'y Int'l L. Proc. 460 to 91 Am. Soc'y Int'l L. Proc. 460, 466 (1997) (Remarks By Anne F. Bayefsky).

[41] Id. at 462-463. Caroline Dommen, *The U.N. Human Rights Regime: Is It Effective?* 91 Am. Soc'y Int'l L. Proc. 460, 462-463 (1997) (Remarks by Thomas Buergenthal) (UN human rights system of web of treaties, meachanisms and instruments seeking to "ratchet-up" human rights).

[42] The fact that individuals have rights and duties under international law is so clear that the more interesting question is whether such rights and duties can be implied in the treaty or must be expressly stated.. See, Jordan J. Paust, Jordan J. Paust, "The Other Side Of Right: Private Duties Under Human Rights Law," 5 *Harv. Hum. Rts. J.* 51 to 5 *Harv. Hum. Rts. J.* 51, 51-52 (1992). Given the state practice of recognizing rights and duties inhering in individuals and the fact that treaties are to be construed liberally the better argument is that it is possible to imply an individual right or duty in the terms of a treaty.

other non-state actors.[43] They usually include an obligation to submit reports[44] to a committee,[45] and a (sometimes optional)[46] right of states against other states and possibly individual rights of action. For example, the Human Rights Committee, the Committee on the Elimination of Racial Discrimination and the Committee against Torture all offer individual complaint procedures.[47] However, these conventions are often subjected to reservations.[48] This process can nevertheless be properly called the constitutionalization of international human rights law, with very different presumptions and goals than the now defunct Westphalian system.[49] This system,[50] an interlocking network of conventions, contributes to the post-Westphalian system of global governance.[51] For example, the function of the International Bill of Rights—i.e. the UDHR, the ICCPR and the CESCR—is to change the behavior of states.[52] The supplementary treaties on race (Convention on the Elimination of Race Discrimination—CERD), [53] gender (Convention on the Elimination of All

---

[43] Monica Pinto, "Fragmentation Or Unification Among International Institutions: Human Rights Tribunals," 31 *N.Y.U. J. Int'l L. & Pol.* 833 to 31 *N.Y.U. J. Int'l L. & Pol.* 833, 833 (1999).

[44] E.g., ICCPR Art. 40 available at: http://www.unhchr.ch/html/menu3/b/a_ccpr.htm.

[45] E.g. ICCPR Art. 28 available at: http://www.unhchr.ch/html/menu3/b/a_ccpr.htm.

[46] E.g., ICCPR Art. 41 available at: http://www.unhchr.ch/html/menu3/b/a_ccpr.htm.

[47] Caroline Dommen, The U.N. Human Rights Regime: Is It Effective? 91 *Am. Soc'y Int'l L. Proc.* 460 to 91 *Am. Soc'y Int'l L. Proc.* 460, 463 (1997) (Remarks By Anne F. Bayefsky). (Remarks By Thomas Buergenthal).

[48] U.S. practice in making extensive reservations to treaties is often criticised. See, e.g.

Frederic L. Kirgis "Reservations to Treaties and United States Practice," *ASIL Insights* (May, 2003) *at:* http://www.asil.org/insights/insigh105.htm.

[49] Nigel David White, *The* United Nations System: Conference, Contract Or Constitutional Order? 4 *Sing. J. Int'l & Comp. L.* 281 to 4 *Sing. J. Int'l & Comp. L.* 281, 298. (2000).

[50] Claire Moore Dickerson, "Human Rights: The Emerging Norm Of Corporate Social Responsibility," 76 *Tul. L. Rev.* 1431 to 76 *Tul. L. Rev.* 1431, 1449 (2002) (Describes UN convention system as democratic global governance).

[51] Jose E. Alvarez, *supra* note 123 at 232-233 (Describes the world as evolving toward institutions and processes of global governance).

[52] Oona A. Hathaway, "Do Human Rights Treaties Make A Difference?" 111 *Yale L.J.* 1935, 1957-1958 (2002) (Describes processes of multilateral treaty making).

[53] International Convention on the Elimination of All Forms of Racial Discrimination,

Forms of Discrimination against Women—CEDAW),[54] and Children[55] similarly seek to change the behavior of states. National courts do regard the decisions, for example of the HRC, as at least persuasive evidence[56] of law[57] and should and sometimes do interpret domestic law as necessarily consistent with international obligations.[58]

The U.N. implementation of human rights[59] is thus one more functionalist success story: Rather than trying to achieve the immediately unattainable, the U.N. has consistently and practically chosen to achieve the possible—all the while seeking to expand the reach of the laws it has sponsored[60] and to ultimately achieve goals which at the time of promul-

---

Mar. 7, 1966, 660 U.N.T.S. 195; available at: http://www.tufts.edu/departments/fletcher/multi/texts/BH490.txt.

[54] *Available at:* http://www.hrweb.org/legal/cdw.html.

[55] Deborah E. Anker "Refugee Law, Gender, And The Human Rights Paradigm," *Harv. Hum. Rts. J.* 133 to 15 Harv. Hum. Rts. J. 133, 134 (2002).

[56] E.C.H.R. cited by the Indian court as evidence of a general principle of law: *Hussainara Khatoon and Others v. Home Secretary,* State of Bihar (1980) 1 SCC 81 (Indian Supreme Court). *But see: Jean v. Nelson,* 727 F.2d 957 (11th Cir. 1984), aff'd on other grounds 105 S. Ct. 2992 (1985) (Custom not found in conventions, resolutions); *Tel Oren v. Libyan Arab Republic,* 726 F. 2d 774 (DC Cir. 1984), cert. denied, 470 U.S. 1003 (1985). *Contrast with: Fernandez Roque v. Smith,* 622 F. Supp. 887 (ND Ga. 1985) modified sub nom. *Fernandez-Roque v. Meese,* 781 F.2d. 1450 (11th Cir. 1986). *See also: Ishtyaq v. Nelson* 627 F. Supp. 13 (EDNY 1983) and *Soroa-Gonz alez v. Civiletti,* 515 F. Supp. 1049 (ND Ga. 1981); Theodor Meron, *Human Rights and Humanitarian Norms as Customary Law,* Oxford: Clarendon at 126 (1989).

[57] Caroline Dommen, *supra* note 50 at 463 (Remarks By Thomas Buergenthal).

[58] See, e.g., *Ram Cahnd Birdi v. Secretary of State for Home Affairs* (1975) 61 *Int'l L. Rep.* (UKCA) 250 (1981) . (Holding that courts must interpret national laws to be consistent with prior international laws because the national legislature is presumed to legislate with international obligations in mind).

[59] Jennifer A. Downs, A Healthy And Ecologically Balanced Environment: An Argument For A Third Generation Right 3 *Duke J. Comp. & Int'l L.* 351, 361 (1993) (Acceptance of human rights into international law occurred via acceptance of UDHR as customary international law and the Covenant on Civil and Political Rights and of the Covenant on Economic, Social, and Cultural Rights).

[60] E.g., Art. 2 ICESCR links human rights protection to economic development and imposes a duty on states to augment the protection of human rights as the state's economic capacity increases: "Each State Party to the present Covenant undertakes to take steps, individually and through international assistance and co-operation, especially economic and technical, to the maximum of its available resources, with a view to achieving progressively the full realization of the rights recognized in the present Covenant by all

gation were unattainable. We can compare this aspect of functionalism to a ratchet: the U.N. has actively pushed to expand and extend human rights[61] and has successfully resisted efforts to restrict or push back those human rights protections which have been achieved. Thus while human rights are still far from secure, the admittedly limited protection human rights offer is constantly albeit gradually expanding.[62]

The conventions generally permit reservations.[63] Enforcement protocols are usually optional.[64] This is to encourage as many states as possible to participate.[65] Permitting reservations and making enforcement protocols optional is defensible because it permits the formation of the *opinio juris*[66] needed to create binding customary international law of which the conventions are evidence.[67]

---

appropriate means, including particularly the adoption of legislative measures." Art. 2 ICESCR available at: http://www.unhchr.ch/html/menu3/b/a_cescr.htm.

[61] E.g., Art. 12 ICESCR states: "1. The States Parties to the present Covenant recognize the right of everyone to the enjoyment of the highest attainable standard of physical and mental health." Thus as technology improves so also does the obligation of the state. ICESCR available at: http://www.unhchr.ch/html/menu3/b/a_cescr.htm.

[62] The obligation of states under the conventions is clear not merely to guarantee existing human rights but also to affirmatively seek to augment the level of protection. For example, Art. 13 ICESCR mandates the progressive introduction of free public higher education, not merely primary and secondary education but also university and technical training. ICESCR Art. 13, available at: http://www.unhchr.ch/html/menu3/b/a_cescr.htm.

[63] With exceptions. E.g., the Optional Protocol to CEDAW specifically prohibits reservations to the protocol. Art. 17, CEDAW Op. Prot. (G.A. res. 54/4, annex, 54 U.N. GAOR Supp. (No. 49) at 5, U.N. Doc. A/54/49 (Vol. I) (2000).

[64] See, e.g., International Covenant on Civil and Political Rights, Dec. 16, 1966, Optional Protocol, 999 U.N.T.S. 302.

[65] Jennifer A. Downs, "A Healthy And Ecologically Balanced Environment: An Argument For A Third Generation Right," 3 *Duke J. Comp. & Int'l L.* 351, 361 (1993) (ICESCR and ICCCPR are binding law). Monica Pinto, "Fragmentation Or Unification Among International Institutions: Human Rights Tribunals," 31 *N.Y.U. J. Int'l L. & Pol.* 833 to 31 *N.Y.U. J. Int'l L. & Pol.* 833, 836 (1999).

[66] *Opinio juris* is found in "verbal statements of governmental representatives to international organizations, in the content of [U.N.] resolutions, declarations, and other normative instruments adopted by such organizations, and in the consent of states to such instruments." Theodor Meron, *supra* note 3 at 42, citing Nicaragua (*Nicaragua v. U.S.*) merits, 1986 ICJ Rep. 14 (Judgement of 27 June).

[67] It must be remembered that customary law is binding upon states, even those states which regard treaties as non-self executing. Military and Paramilitary Activities in and

How does the U.N. "ratchet" up human rights? International human rights law often finds its origin as universal ideals—not as binding law. These ideals however are expressed in non-binding universal instruments.[68] This is not always merely hypocritical whitewash of brutal realities:[69] universal non-binding instruments are promulgated in order to form the *opinio juris* of an international custom[70] which ripens into customary law.[71] The ideals presented in human rights declarations, resolutions and conventions represent moral goals and standards which cannot be resisted because of their universal appeal and legitimising power: democracy—or at least popular consent—is in theory the legitimating norm[72] *sine qua non* of almost all regimes. Even undemocratic ones are attracted to universalist human rights ideals. Thus, in practice, international human rights norms are identified by the U.N. in hortatory declarations such as the Universal Declaration of Human Rights.[73] These hor-

---

against Nicaragua (*Nicar. v. U.S.*) *id*. NB: customary international law is, unlike treaty law, regarded by the United States as self executing. This also explains the vitality of customary international law even in this era of conventional systems such as the WTO and UN. Jordan J. Paust, "Customary International Law And Human Rights Treaties Are Law Of The United States," 20 *Mich. J. Int'l L.* 301 to 20 *Mich. J. Int'l L.* 301, 336 (1999). *Opinio juris* can arise out of U.N. General Assembly resolutions and Conventions Meron, *supra* note 3 at 86.

[68] Thus the conventions are open to all U.N. member states, state parties to the statute of the ICJ, and any other state the Generaly Assembly of the U.N. invites. E.g. ICCPR Art. 48, http://www.unhchr.ch/html/menu3/b/a_ccpr.htm; ICESCR Art. 26 *available at:* http://www.unhchr.ch/html/menu3/b/a_cescr.htm.

[69] There is of course plenty of hypocrisy in international relations. See e.g., Gabe Varges, *The New International Economic Order Legal Debate,* p. 1 (Peter Lang, Frankfurt 1983).

[70] *The North Sea Continental Shelf Cases* (FRG/Den.; FRG Neth.), 1969 ICJ Rep. 3, 44 (Judgment of 20 Feb.) stated that international law defines custom as a universal or near universal state practice coupled with a sense of legal obligation.

[71] But Bin Cheng, argues against the transformationist thesis that international custom can be constituted from international conventions. Bin Cheng, "Custom: The Future of General State Practice in a Divided World" in R. Macdonald, D. Johnston (eds.) *The Structure and Process of International Law: Essays in Legal Philosophy Doctrine and Theory* (Martinus Nijhof,. 1986), 515.

[72] The right to democracy is also guaranteed in the U.N. convention system. Thus, e.g. Art. 21, Art 25 (a) ICCPR, Art. 1 ICESCR, Art. 4 ICESCR.

[73] Richard Klein, "Cultural Relativism, Economic Development And International Human Rights In The Asian Context", 9 *Touro Int'l L. Rev.* 1 to 9 *Touro Int'l L. Rev.* 1,

tatory declarations "merely" identify goals—of the entire global community.

Non-binding human rights goals and ideals constitute *opinio juris*[74]—one element of customary law.[75] States believe that they "ought" to observe human rights and that is the *opinio juris* needed to form customary international law[76] as evidenced by signature to the instruments or silence in the face of universal adoption of the instruments.[77]

States could present themselves as a persistent objector[78] and avoid being the subject of any customary law, which later might develop out of those norms. However, to be a persistent objector a state must openly, notoriously and objectively manifest its dissent to the international custom[79] *ab initio*. No state can do this and retain credibility and legitimacy in the international arena: No state wishes to go on record as favoring torture. No state wishes to affirm the inferior status of women. No state will admit to being racist—because to do so would be to delegitimate that state. The idea of human rights is in fact so attractive that it is literally impossible for all but the most tyrannical of states to deny their exis-

---

1-2 (2001) (Rise of human rights a conscious rejection of the former state system due to world wars).

[74] Some argue, erroneously, that *opinio* is logically the only element needed to constitute international custom. See Bin Cheng "Custom: The Future of General State Practice in a Divided World" in R. Macdonald, D. Johnston (eds.) *supra* note 84 at 530-531.

[75] Other elements than *opinio juris* and practice may be needed to form customary international law. In describing national customary law, the eminent judge Blackstone noted that custom must: "(1) have been 'used so long, that the memory of man runneth not to the contrary'; (2) be continued without interruption; (3) be peaceably acquiesced (4) be reasonable; (5) be certain in its terms; (6) be accepted as compulsory; and (7) be consistent with other customs." Jo Lynn Slama, "Opinio Juris In Customary International Law," 15 *Okla. City U. L. Rev.* 610, (1990).

[76] Ivan Poullaos, "The Nature Of The Beast: Using The Alien Tort Claims Act To Combat International Human Rights Violations," 80 *Wash. U. L.Q.* 327, 333 (2002) (custom with *opinio juris* can ripen from a mere practice into international customary law).

[77] Customary law can evolve "without express universal consent." Jo Lynn Slama, "Opinio Juris In Customary International Law," 15 *Okla. City U. L. Rev.* 626, (1990).

[78] Custom may arise out of acquiescence by non-signatories, i.e. absence of objective objection. Theodor Meron, *supra* note 3 at 89.

[79] The principle of the "persistent objector" in international law provides that a state is not bound to a rule of customary law where it has expressly and persistently objected to that rule. Jo Lynn Slama, *supra* note 88 at 627.

tence.[80] Thus there are rarely if ever persistent objectors to the normative goals of the hortatory declarations of human rights.

States support human rights not merely for defensive legitimation purposes but also for instrumentalist reasons of *Realpolitik*.[81] Human rights can be an instrument of foreign policy.[82] States which support human rights have thereby a weapon. That weapon may be weak. It may be readily discarded. However, the weapon of human rights can be wielded in surprising context which appear, at first glance, to have nothing to do with human rights.[83] U.S.-Chinese trade is but one example where even if human rights are used only as a pretext for substantive goals they are nevertheless supported and defended.[84] No state wishes to renounce a potential tool in its diplomatic toolkit. The cost of observing most human rights is relatively low. Consequently states observe human rights and even claim to promulgate them for reasons of *Realpolitik*.[85] States do not reject human rights norms because to do so would deny them the ability

---

[80] Paul W. Kahn, "American Hegemony And International Law Speaking Law To Power: Popular Sovereignty, Human Rights, And The New International Order," 1 *Chi. J. Int'l L.* 1, 12 (2000) (All modern states combine democracy and human rights).

[81] Daniel W. Drezner, "On The Balance Between International Law And Democratic Sovereignty," 2 *Chi. J. Int'l L.* 321 to 2 *Chi. J. Int'l L.* 321 (2001), (notes the *Realpolitik* nature of human rights law).

[82] For example, President James Carter made human rights a key plank in his foreign policy. Harlan Cleveland, "Introduction: The Chain Reaction of Human Rights." In Alice Henkin (ed.), *Human Dignity: The Internationalization of Human Rights,* (New York: Aspen Institute, 1979), p. ix.

[83] William C. Plouffe, *supra* note 38 at 79; also *see:* Lois E. Fielding, "Taking The Next Step In The Development Of New Human Rights: The Emerging Right Of Humanitarian Assistance To Restore Democracy," 5 *Duke J. Comp. & Int'l L.* 329, 329 (1995) (supporting humanitarian intervention in Haiti). For "surprising contexts" see e.g. Lisa L. Bhansali, "New Customary Law: Taking Human Rights Seriously?" 87 *Am. Soc'y Int'l L. Proc.* 229 to 87 *Am. Soc'y Int'l L. Proc.* 229, 240 (1993) which discusses a case where two rival warlords in the Horn of Africa were intent on mutual destruction without regard to civilian casualties until the reality that as a consequence whoever would win would have no credibility in the outside world.

[84] For a concise compelling account of the use of human rights in statecraft verifying the customary nature of international human rights instruments including the UDHR and the ICCPR *see:* Louis B. Sohn, *supra* note 5 at 16.

[85] Thus, for example, U.S. foreign policy is unilateralist only when unilateralism serves U.S. interests.

to criticize other states credibly when those other states violate human rights. Human rights acquire the *opinio juris* needed to ripen into customary law for the above mentioned reasons.[86]

2. Enforcement of Global Norms: State Practice

Opinio juris is only one element of customary international law. The other aspect is state practice. For a custom to become binding law it must in practice be obeyed and considered to be obligatory. State practice in national law of the developed world upholds the international human rights norms. Internationally, the U.N. conventions also are practices of states to recognize international human rights: The ICCRP[87] and ICESCR[88] as well as the CEDAW and CAT include optional enforcement clauses and/or optional enforcement protocols. Thus practice grows over time by national law and under international law to create customary human rights law ratcheting up global standards.

3. Individual Rights

The U.N. convention system (ICCPR, ICESCR, CEDAW, CAT, CERD etc.) constitutes part of a global system of functionalist governance[89] which breaks from the Westphalian model of states as hermetic monopolists of legitimate authority by recognizing rights inhering in individuals.[90] International law seeks to impose order rather than justice,[91] but is evolving toward putting justice before order as can be seen in the third

---

[86] Even the United States recognizes that non-binding norms may evolve into custom. "norms ... may ripen in the future into rules of customary international law." H.R. Rep. No. 102-367, at 4 (1991), reprinted in 1992 U.S.C.C.A.N. 84, 86.

[87] International Covenant on Civil and Political Rights, Dec. 16, 1966, Optional Protocol, 999 U.N.T.S. 302.

[88] International Covenant on Economic, Social and Cultural Rights, Dec. 16, 1966 993 U.N.T.S. 3.

[89] Ulrich K. Preuss, "The Force, Frailty, And Future Of Human Rights Under Globalization," 1 *Theoretical Inquiries L.* 283, 304 (2000) (Argues that the international community is in transition from nation state to global community).

[90] Jose E. Alvarez *The New Treaty Makers* 25 B. C. Int'l. & Comp. L.Rev. 213, 216 (2002). *Available at:* http://www.bc.edu/bc_org/avp/law/lwsch/journals/bciclr/25_2/03_FMS.htm.

[91] "the goal of international law-namely the achievement of a stable, just international order"

generation rights to democracy, peace and development, the rights to humanitarian assistance, humanitarian intervention and the right to national self determination.[92] Recent case law recognizes that both natural and legal persons owe duties under international law toward other individuals (*Flick*;[93] *Krupp* [94]) and have rights against individuals (*Marcos*[95]; Alien Tort Statute) both in civil (*Kadic v Karadzic*)[96]and penal law (*Eichmann*).[97] The principle of sovereignty has declined at exactly the same moment as the principle of universal human rights has risen.

B. THE UNIVERSALITY OF HUMAN RIGHTS[98]

The idea of human rights at first seems vague and ambiguous.[99] For this very reason the idea has a universal appeal, being all things to all

---

Lucas W. Andrews, "Sailing Around The Flat Earth: The International Tribunal For The Former Yugoslavia As A Failure Of Jurisprudential Theory," 11 *Emory Int'l L. Rev.* 471, 513 (1997).

[92] Gudmundur Alfredsson, "The United Nations And Human Rights," 25 *Int'l J. Legal Info.* 17, 21 (1997). U.N. Charter arts. 1, 2, 55.

[93] *U.S. v. Flick and Others,* 9 War Crimes Reports 1.

[94] *U.S. v. Krupp and Others,* 10 War Crimes Reports 69.

[95] *In re Estate of Ferdinand E. Marcos Human Rts. Litia.,* 978 F.2d 493 (9th Cir. 1992).

[96] *Kadic v. Karadzic* (Part III: Justiciability) discusses in detail the requirements of the political question doctrine. Note that in *Kadic* no political question was found. *Kadic v. Karadzic,* 70 F.3d 232 (2d Cir. 1996), cert. denied 518 US 1005 (1996) *available at:*
http://www.yale.edu/lawweb/avalon/diana/karadzic/4298-12.html.

[97] Interestingly, *Eichmann* is not the only case where a national was kidnapped in a foreign state by a prosecuting state but had no remedy because the remedy was held by the state where he was kidnapped from. *See:* Crim. 4 juin 1964, *Argoud,* JCP. 1964, II, 13806, rapport Comte (France: Cour de Cassation, Chambre Criminelle). *See also:* Brigette Belton Homrig, "Abduction As An Alternative To Extradition—A Dangerous Method To Obtain Jurisdiction Over Criminal Defendants," 28 *Wake Forest L. Rev.* 671 (1993). Manuel Noriega also complained of abduction in *U.S. v. Noriega,* 117 F.3d 1206 to 117 F.3d 1206, 1222 (11th Cir. 1997)—and just as unsuccessfully.

[98] Some argue that the incoherence within human rights is inherent in the concept of human rights and not merely due to cultural splits: Ruti Teitel, "Human Rights Genealogy," 66 *Fordham L. Rev.* 301, 302 (1997) (Arguing that the dualisms and ambiguity of international human rights law can be resolved via resort to history).

[99] John King Gamble, Teresa A. Bailey, Jared S. Hawk, Erin E. McCurdy, "Human Rights Treaties: A Suggested Typology, An Historical Perspective," 7 *Buff. Hum. Rts. L. Rev.* 33, 34 (2001) (Ineluctability of human rights).

men. Though problematic, the claim of human rights to universality is valid.[100] Globalism and universalism can in theory be complementary and correlate in practice.[101] Humanists point to the common needs and aspirations of all persons as evidence of a common humanity which is the foundation of universal rights. Universal human rights are a key feature of the post-Westphalian state system.[102]Despite theoretical confusion and cultural clashwhich obscure their sources, resulting in difficulty in defining rights, the idea of human rights is indeed universal and is a key feature of the post-Westphalian order.[103]

Our first demonstration of the universality of human rights is a negative proof.[104] The universality of human rights is demonstrated by the very existence of these debates. Were human rights not a universal con-

---

[100] For a discussion of how human rights may be a tool of western imperialism see, Johan Galtung, *The Universality of Human Rights Revisited: Some Less Applaudable Consequences of the Human Rights Tradition* in *Human Rights in Perspective*, Asbjorn Eide, Bernt Hagtvet, Oxford: Blackwell (1992) *at* 152 (arguing that human rights are not only a key to liberation but also a vector of state control).

[101] Peter Fitzpatrick *Globalization and the Humanity of Rights*, 2000 (1) Law, Social Justice and Global Development (LGD). *at:* ttp://elj.warwick.ac.uk/global/issue/2000-1/fitzpatrick.html (Arguing that globalism, like human rights, is a universalist ideology. Thus globalism permits human rights to escape the limits of the nation state).

[102] The universality debate has been presented as a "clash of civilizations". Its history has been summarised as follows: (describing the debates between the 'politics of universalism' and the 'politics of difference.' and 'identity politics' in international criminal law. basis of group affiliation.) Martha C. Nussbaum, "In Defense Of Universal Value," 36 *Idaho L. Rev.* 379, 447 (2000).

[103] Brenda Cossman, "Reform, Revolution, Or Retrenchment? International Human Rights In The Post-Cold War Era," 32 *Harv. Int'l L.J.* 339 to 32 *Harv. Int'l L.J.* 339, 340 (1991) (Rights are superior in the hierarchy of norms because they are universal in space and time). Jennifer Nedelsky, "Communities Of Judgment And Human Rights," 1 *Theoretical Inquiries L.* 245, 245 (2000) (Universality debate must be seen as a discourse between different communities). Makau Wa Mutua, "The Ideology Of Human Rights," 36 *Va. J. Int'l L.* 589, 589-590 (1996) (Human rights are ambiguous as to their scope, content, and philosophical bases). John King Gamble, Teresa A. Bailey, Jared S. Hawk, Erin E. McCurdy, *supra* note 116 *at* 34. (Ineluctability of human rights). Antonio Cassese, *supra* note 2 at 51 (Argues that universality is a myth).

[104] "The concept of the universality of human rights is based on the notion th*at:* (a) there is a universal human nature; (b) this human nature is knowable; (c) it is knowable by reason; and (d) human nature is essentially different from other reality." Yash Gha, "Universalism And Relativism: Human Rights As A Framework For Negotiating Interethnic Claims," 21 *Cardozo L. Rev.* 1094, 1096 (2000) *available at:* http://www.cardozo.yu.edu/cardlrev/v21n4/ghai.pdf.

cept these debates would not exist. This negative proof of the universality of human rights is not the only one.[105] A more ambitious affirmative demonstration of the universality of human rights is also possible.[106] A neo-Aristotelian understanding of human nature posits a mutually reinforcing relationship between human rights and the rule of law and (unlike Aristotle) gender and racial equality.[107] But this relationship is determined not by the formal legalism of the rule of law. Rather, it is determined by the substantive achievements of human rights—whether those rights function as a means to obtain and secure what Aristotle termed "the good life."[108] Human rights are thus a means to the end of political society which ensure and obtain not merely life, but the good life for the members of the polity.[109] It is for this reason that human rights are universal[110]— humans have universally common capacities, needs, and desires and an interest in prospering. Human rights are the means to a universally desired end, the good life.

A pragmatic argument for the universality of human rights is also possible. The universality of human rights is a legal fact recognized by international law.[111] This argument, like the first argument that human rights must exist since everyone is talking about them, is not alone par-

---

[105] Another negative proof is the fact that while the contents of the rights are disputed their existence is not. Some even go so far as to venture to isolate a "common core" of human rights at the global level reflected from national law. See, L. Amede Obiora, "Reconstituted Consonants: The Reach Of A "Common Core" Analogy In Human Rights," 21 *Hastings Int'l & Comp. L. Rev.* 921 to 21 *Hastings Int'l & Comp. L. Rev.* 921, 955 (1998).

[106] Antonio Cassese, *supra* note 2 at 64 (argues for the existence of a common core of human rights recognized globally).

[107] Samuel P. Hunting *The Clash of Civilizations and the Remaking of World Order* (1996) p. 70.

[108] E.g., Aristoteles, Nikomachische Ethik, Buch I, Kap. 2,3, 5. Available at: http://www.unirostock.de/fakult/philfak/fkw/iph/strobach/hroseminare/mkethik/arist1.pdf.

[109] Aristotle, *Politics,* (c. 350 b.c.) Book I, Part II *available at:* http://classics.mit.edu/Aristotle/politics.1.one.html.

[110] It is also for this reason that human rights are inherently cosmopolitan and international. Robin West, "Is The Rule Of Law Cosmopolitan?" 19 *QLR* 259, 259 (2000).

[111] Elsa Stamatopoulou, "The Development Of United Nations Mechanisms For The Protection And Promotion Of Human Rights," 55 *Wash. & Lee L. Rev.* 687 to 55 *Wash. & Lee L. Rev.* 687, 692 (1998).

ticularly strong. Even tyrants assert the justice of their tyranny. However the negative argument and the practical argument complement and strengthen the teleological argument. This argument can be further strengthened by inquiring into the nature of rights.

1. Rights and Duties

For every right there is a corresponding duty.[112] I have a right to life and you have a duty not to kill me. The third world believes in human rights too and the sponsored "New International Economic Order" (NIEO),[113] by a resolution before the U.N. General Assembly in 1974,[114] proposed a charter of economic rights and duties.[115] Third world scholars accept the idea of economic development, one of the keystones of modernity, as the *sine qua non* of existence.[116]

The question whether rights arise from duties is seen in Asian schools of thought,[117] whether Islamic,[118]

---

[112] Mahatma Gandhi, from *Yervada Mandir* (1930), *excerpt at:* http://meadev.nic.in/Gandhi/economics.htm; H.R. Khanna, *Rule of Law*, 4 SCC (Jour) 7 (1977) *Available at:* http://www.ebc-india.com/lawyer/articles/77v4a3.htm. This principle has also been recognized in the case law. *See, e.g., Medical Review Committee v Lim* (1981), 8 Man. R. (2d) 407 (Q.B.). (Canada, province of Manitoba).

[113] *See* Gabe Varges *supra* note 82 at 5.

[114] *See* Claude Nigoul, Maurice Torrelli , *Les Mystifications du Nouvel Ordre International*, p. 105 (Paris: PUF, 1982).

[115] *See* Gabe Varges, *supra* note 82 at 17.

[116] Tesfatsion Medhanie, "Lomé: Can it help reverse Africa's marginalization?" in Peter Meyns (ed.), 16 *Staat und Gesellschaft in Afrika*. 397, 402 (1996).

[117] This view is not however without critique: See e.g., Michael C. Davis, "Constitutionalism And Political Culture: The Debate Over Human Rights And Asian Values," 11 *Harv. Hum. Rts. J*. 109, 147 (1998). And see Antonio Cassese, *supra* note 2 at 53.

[118] There is no absence of Islamic scholarship in the west on this topic. Further the Islamic scholars do not question the idea of human rights as such but rather the western view of what those rights are. See e.g. Ebrahim Moosa, "The Dilemma Of Islamic Rights Schemes," 15 *J.L. & Religion* 185, 215 (2000); Ann Mayer "Universal Versus Islamic Human Rights: A Clash Of Cultures Or A Clash With A Construct?" 15 *Mich. J. Int'l L.* 307, 307 (1994); Abdulaziz Othman Altwaijri, *Human Rights in Islamic Teachings*, p. 4 (2000) *available at:* http://www.isesco.org.ma/pub/Eng/humanrights/page.htm.

Hindu,[119] Confucian,[120] or Buddhist.[121] Both Eastern and South Asian cultures tend to see not rights but rather duties as primary, and to recognize rights only as a consequence of duty fulfilled.[122] In contrast, western schools of thought, notably *ius naturale*,[123] tend to see the foundation of human rights on certain inalienable inherent capacities of humans,[124] generally speaking rationality, though Christian theologianswould combine that theory with the idea that that rationality is a reflection of divine perfection.[125]

Ius naturale is generally contrasted with positivism,[126] not only in national law but also in international law.[127] Purvis traces that split to the treaty of Westphalia.[128] However, the opposition of positivism to naturalism is usually inexact and often leads to confusion.[129] Sohn concise-

---

[119] Editorial, *Human Rights: Knots and Webs,* Hinduism Today (1996) *available at:* http://www.hinduism-today.com/1996/6/1996-6-07.html.

[120] Joseph Chan "Human Rights and Confucian Virtues," *IV Harvard Asia Qtly.* (2000) *available at:* http://www.fas.harvard.edu/~asiactr/haq/200003/0003a006.htm.

[121] Damien Keown, "Are There 'Human Rights' in Buddhism?" 2 *Journal of Buddhist Ethics* (1995) *available at:* http://www.urbandharma.org/udharma/humanrights.html.

[122] See, e.g. Mahatma Gandhi, "Letter to the Director General of Unesco, 25 May 1947," IV *Human Rights Teaching* 4 (1985).

[123] See, e.g. Alfred Verdross and Heribert Franz Koeck *Natural Law: The Tradition of Universal Reason and Authority* in R. Macdonald, D. Johnston (eds.) *supra* note 21 *at* 17.

[124] See, e.g. "South West Africa Cases (*Ethiopia v. South Africa; Liberia v. South Africa*)" *ICJ Reports* 1966 p. 250 (297) (dissenting opinion of Judge Tanaka). But see Dr. H. Agarwal, "Implementation of Human Rights Covenants with Special Reference to India," pp. 17-18 (1983) (arguing that human rights are universal because they arise out of the common equality of all persons).

[125] Thomas Aquinas, *Summa Theologica,* Secunda Secundae Partis §57 (Right) *available at*: http://www.newadvent.org/summa/3.htm. Fr. Joseph M. de Torre, "Human Rights, Natural Law, And Thomas Aquinas," VI *Catholic Social Scientist Review*, (2001) *available at:* http://www.catholicsocialscientists.org/Article—deTorre—Human%20Rights.htm.

[126] For a brief brilliant summary of the (only illusory) contradiction between natural law and positivism by the late Louis B. Sohn, see, Louis B. Sohn, *supra* note 5 at 17 (1982).

[127] Nigel Purvis "Critical Legal Studies In Public International Law," 32 *Harv. Int'l L.J.* 94, at 81-83, (1991) (Describes "naturalist" "positivist" dichotomy in international law).

[128] Nigel Purvis *id. at* 82-83. (Describes the supposed decline of *ius naturale* theory).

[129] Unless the two schools of thought take a great deal of care to define their starting

ly demonstrates that the splits between positivism and natural law are complementary[130] because natural law concerns inalienable rights, and positive law concerns alienable rights.[131] He concludes that those elements of international law which are *jus cogens* are a reflection of natural law, whereas those human rights that are derogable are a reflection of positive law.[132] For Aristotle, nature (*physis*) concerns that which is unchangeable (i.e. natural law), that which cannot be otherwise; in contrast *tekhne* (gr.) or *arte* (lat.)—that which can be other than it is (i.e. man made, or positive law). Sohn and Aristotle see that natural law concerns that which is universal and unchanging and positive law concerns that which can be different in different times and places. Rubin, in contrast, describes those schisms but does not synthesize them.[133] Determining where one stands on these dividing line questions is a matter of science, not of opinion. A scientific position is an objective reflection of material facts—not a subjective expression of feelings.

Scientificity of law is sometimes challenged—though generally only implicitly—by postmodern denials of the existence of objectivity, truth, and *in ultimo* western culture (its existence and/or values). These denials permit PoMo to pose radical questions such as why roughly 80 percent of the world controls roughly 20 percent of its resources and whether war is inevitable. However in rejecting objectivity—and thus knowledge—PoMo throws out the good with the bad. Because of its presumptions PoMo cannot benefit from the earlier work of any social theory. For the postmodernist, objectivity does not and cannot exist. It is thus difficult to take the postmodernists seriously: their presumptions are contrary to common sense. But one must take postmodernism seriously because the postmoderns' denial of basic presumptions of modernity such as objectivity, science and progress permits them to pose serious questions. Yet the rejection of the presumptions of modernity pre-

---

point, they find themselves talking about quite different things. Nigel Purvis id. at 115, (1991).

[130] Louis B. Sohn, *supra* note 5 at 17.

[131] *Id.*

[132] *Id.*

[133] Alfred P. Rubin, *Actio Popularis, Jus Cogens And Offenses Erga Omnes?*, 35 New Eng. L. Rev. 265, 280, (2001).

vents postmodernists from forming coherent answers to the fundamental questions which they pose.

Hobbes reconciles positive and natural law by proposing that natural law is nothing other than the law of the jungle, the law of the strong, survival of the fittest.[134] An alternative school of *ius naturalis* (put forward most famously by Cicero,[135] and later Aquinas[136]) argues that only laws which are founded in morality and/or rationality are valid. I regard the former theory (Hobbes) as natural law (per Hobbes, *lex naturalis*), and the latter (Cicero and Aquinas) as natural justice. Both are branches of *ius non scripta*.

Just as there is a descriptive and prescriptive theory of *ius non scripta* (natural law and natural justice respectively) there are also descriptive and prescriptive versions of positivism (*ius scripta*). Descriptive positivism limits itself to describing law as it is. Prescriptive positivism does not prescribe what the law should be; rather it describes what it perceives as correct methods of legal science. Kelsen,[137] following Weber[138] is an example of a prescriptive positivist. Much of the supposed conflict between positivism and naturalism can be resolved by correctly understanding which strand of theory one is considering. Prescriptive theories of natural law are necessarily in conflict with prescriptive theories of positivism. Purely descriptive theories, however, cannot be in methodological conflict since they only claim to describe reality as it is.

As Nigel Purvis notes, the claim that positivism is purely descrip-

---

[134] "the condition of man (as hath been declared in the precedent chapter) is a condition of war of every one against every one, in which case every one is governed by his own reason, and there is nothing he can make use of that may not be a help unto him in preserving his life against his enemies". Hobbes, *Leviathan* Ch. XIV (1656). Hobbes also distinguishes between natural law and natural right. *Id.*

[135] Cicero, *The Republic* at *III, XXII* (Loeb Classical Library, 1950). *Available at:* http://www.thelatinlibrary.com/cicero/repub.shtml (lat.).

[136] Thomas Aquinas, *Summa Theologica,* Secunda Secundae Partis §57 (Right) *available at*: http://www.newadvent.org/summa/3.htm supra note 161.

[137] See, e.g. Hans Kelsen, *Allgemeine Staatslehre* (1925).

[138] Max Weber, *Der Sinn der „Wertfreiheit" der soziologischen und ökonomischen Wissenschaften* (1917). In: Ders.: *Gesammelte Aufsätze zur Wissenschaftslehre.* Tübingen 1988.

tive explains some of its success in capturing legal imagination.[139] Most natural law theories, with the notable exception of Hobbes,[140] are in fact theories of natural justice and as such are prescriptive. Natural law theorists often do not distinguish prescription from description. Since a descriptive positivism has a more limited task than a prescriptive naturalism it necessarily generates a simpler theory which is less open to critique, but which is descriptively incomplete (no cognition of whole entities, i.e. the sum is always equal and never greater than its parts thus no synergies)[141] and is essentially powerless because it does not prescribe. Positivism, like IR "realism," pursues a much less ambitious theoretical objective than naturalism or holism but for this very reason is also less influential. In contrast, the grander objectives of naturalist and holist theories make it likelier that failures in those theories will be glaringly obvious. Such grand errors are generally due to "pure" *eidetic noesis*, i.e. philosophical idealism, divorced from material reality. Positivist theories in contrast are confined to safer materialist descriptions and thus less likely to fail catastrophically.[142]

---

[139] Nigel Purvis *supra* note 290 *at* 81-83, (1991) (Describes the naturalist riposte to positivism).

[140] Hobbes clearly describes a natural law theory—but his natural law is the law of the jungle which like Rousseau must be escaped by a social contract, i.e. a positive law: "The right of nature, which writers commonly call *jus naturale*, is the liberty each man hath to use his own power as he will himself for the preservation of his own nature; that is to say, of his own life; and consequently, of doing anything which, in his own judgement and reason, he shall conceive to be the aptest means thereunto." Thomas Hobbes, *Leviathan,* Ch. XIV (1660) *available at:* http://www.orst.edu/instruct/phl302/texts/hobbes/leviathan-contents.html. The work of both Hobbes and Rousseau (and Locke for that matter) is however flawed because they presume an impossibility, namely the state of nature. Hobbes's theory of natural law — the law of the jungle, *droit de plus fort*, does however carefully distinguish between natural law and natural right and thus should be distinguished from other theories of natural law which usually do not make this distinction and thus confuse prescription and description.

[141] Perhaps the first and best known example of a synergy arising where a whole is greater than the sum of its parts is Adam Smith's famous needle factory. Smith pointed out that a factory using laborers specialised in different tasks would be far more efficient at needle production than the same number of individuals working in isolation. Adam Smith, *An Inquiry into the Nature and Causes of the Wealth of Nations*, B.I, Ch.1, "Of the Division of Labor", in paragraph I.1.3 (1776). *Available at:* http://www.econlib.org/library/Smith/smWN1.html.

[142] See Purvis, *supra* note 290.

Methodologically, the split between positivism and naturalism tracks and parallels the splits between materialism and idealism, between atomism and holism and between realism and transformationism.[143] However, though materialism, atomism, positivism and realism tend to be reinforcing and though historically holism and idealism are usually associated with each other, the connection of these different theories to each other is not a necessary one. This author for example takes a holistic materialistic view that compels him to a transformationist theory. Hobbes, in contrast, is a materialist atomist who takes a position of natural law—though his "natural law" is in fact, the law of the jungle![144] Only by expressing these theoretical differences and clearly delineating them can post-Westphalian theorists hope to transcend the failures and limitations of Westphalian state theory.

This relation between positivism and natural justice contextualizes and guides this paper's theory of human rights. The rights and duties theories appear at first to present a fundamentally irreconcilable duality. However, though there are mutually exclusive dualities, there are also dualities which are in fact not absolutely opposite and mutually exclusive (discontinuous entities) but rather which are different not in kind but in degree. Such dualities are continuous entities.[145] An atomist must believe that the universe is discontinuous since only discontinuous entities resolve into discrete elements. Holists see the universe as a continuous whole where each microcosm reflects the macrocosm. The aporia of light as both a particle and wave may be a useful analogy or model to understand this split. A mathematical model may also help. Currently

---

[143] For a good discussion of different methodologies *see:* Anne-Marie Slaughter, Steven R. Ratner, "The Method Is The Message" 93 *Am. J. Int'l L.* 410 (1999).

[144] In fairness to Hobbes, we must note that his first natural law, the law of self preservation, by any means necessary, is only his point of departure. He goes on to develop other consequential rights which he considers just as "natural" as the right of self preservation. E.g. *pacta sunt servanda, (inter alia).* Thomas Hobbes, *Leviathan,* Ch. XV "Of Other Laws of Nature" (1660) *available at:* http://www.orst.edu/instruct/phl302/texts/hobbes/leviathan-c.html#CHAPTER XV.

[145] To understand the theoretical distinctions between analog and digital conceptualization *see:* Gottfried Leibniz, *A new method for maxima and minima as well as tangents, which is impeded neither by fractional nor by irrational quantities, and a remarkable type of calculus for this* (1684), Isaac Newton, *Fluxions* (1666 - then unpublished working paper, later published), Isaac Newton, *Analysis With Infinite Series* (1711).

mathematics is seen as a purely arbitrary formal system and no reflection of reality. Historically however, mathematics has been seen, at least since Pythagoras, as a reflection of reality. If mathematics were a reflection of reality then the existence of irrational numbers such as radical two implies that reality is not discontinuous and that the holists, not the atomists, are correct. The holist theory is more accurate because a discontinuous world explains the existence of paradoxical ratios such as the square root of two. In contrast the atomist representation of discontinuous discrete atoms cannot adequately describe irrational numbers or repeating numbers.

If ideas are merely a reflection of material reality (and not a formal system divorced from material reality) then the atomist view, that the universe can be divided into ultimate discrete elements which cannot be further subdivided and which serve as the fundamental basis of analysis is incorrect. We can always imagine an ever smaller point which is why geometry presumes that any line segment is made of an infinite number of points—atomists in contrast presume that that process of division must end somewhere. But let us assume, for the sake of argument, the opposite position, that the universe is a discontinuous whole. As such we could presume, as integral calculus does, the possibility of an infinite series converging upon a limit. The presumption of continuity—which, like radical two is paradoxical—is consistent with holism and leads to empirically verifiable and useful conclusions. The presumption of discontinuity leads to contradiction. Consequently the holist position is again better able to represent reality and is probably more correct than the atomist position. This argument of course relies on the materialist presumption that ideas reflect material reality and do not exist independent from material reality. It also relies on the presumption—which again is not the presumption of modern mathematics—that mathematics, like any idea, is a reflection of material reality and thus not a purely formal system.

Pointing out the mathematical deficiencies in atomism is not intended to say that there is no place for analysis in scientific thought. It is rather intended to temper the role that such analysis is given in a comprehensive theory. Obviously both continuity and discontinuity have their place in mathematics. The fact that holism can consistently integrate atomism as a special theory and maintain the presumptions of holism as a general theory explains why it is the more powerful theory, especially when based in materialism.

The contradiction between rights theories ("western" theories) and duties theories ("eastern" theories) of human rights is only apparent. Both western and eastern schools of thought are connected parts of a continuous whole linked by the common term: humanity. As expressions of degrees of continuity these apparent opposites are in fact reconcilable. An eastern Taoist perspective sees two connected opposites transforming into each other. A western view reaches that same unity of opposites and mutual transformation of opposites into each other through dialectical materialism. Though Taoism is a precursor to dialectical materialism they differ. Unlike dialectical materialism Taoism is not materialist, but idealist. Further, unlike dialectical materialism Taoism does not account for historical progress, the tendency of systems to greater complexity over time. Taoism is a good start but not the end.

Looking back at western thinkers, when we explore the thought of Plato, he clearly postulates duties as primary in his Republic.[146] To the extent that Aristotle acknowledges the idea of "right" (and thus of "rights")[147] he posits them as a consequence of human rationality.[148] But Aristotle's conception of rights is balanced by his understanding of the inherently social nature of humans. For Aristotle, like Rousseau, the state finds its origins in the family and, unlike its individual members, the state (an extended family) is self sufficient.[149] Because the state is

---

[146] Plato, *Republic* Book IV *available at:* http://classics.mit.edu/Plato/republic.5.iv.html.

[147] Aristotle does speak of "civil rights" i.e. *Bürgerrechte*; Aristotle, *Athenian Constitution*—Part 7, Sections 6—69 (Translated by Sir Frederic G. Kenyon) *available at:*

http://www.ekloges.com.cy/nqcontent.cfm?tt=article&a_id=1540.

[148] This can be seen by the example of the slave : Aristotle regards the slave as only capable of apprehending but not forming ideas. Aristotle, *Politics*, Book I, Part 5, Para. 3 (c. 350 b.c) *available at*: http://classics.mit.edu/Aristotle/politics.1.one.html supra note 164. Consequently the slave has few rights. However the slave, like the drunkard, also has fewer duties, and for a similar reason—at least per Aristotle. What was the practice actually like though? Supra note 164.

[149] "La plus ancienne de toutes les sociétés et la seule naturelle est celle de la famille. ... La famille est donc si l'on veut le premier modèle des sociétés politiques" Jean Jacques Rousseau, *Contrat Social* (1762), Livre I, Chapitre II. *available at:* http://un2sg4.unige.ch/athena/rousseau/jjr_cont.html#L1/2.

self-sustaining it has priority over any one of its members.[150] Thus, Aristotle's conception of rights, like Rousseau's, would necessarily contextualize rights by the society in which they are found. Indeed it is only relatively late in western thought that that we see Locke present the possibility of rights divorced from society. Locke's labor theory of value permits an a-social man, because property according to Locke is not a social relation but the consequence of individual labor[151]—which is empirically defensible (as well as being the position of Karl Marx)[152]— unlike the subjective theories of value offered by Rothbard[153] and Mises[154] or the postmodernists. Admittedly, roots of theoretical atomism can also be found in Hobbes[155] and even Rousseau.[156] But it is only with Locke that the individual can be divorced from society because proper-

---

[150] See Aristotle, *Politics,* Book I Part II (Translated by Benjamin Jowett) *available at*: http://classics.mit.edu/Aristotle/politics.1.one.html. *supra* note 164.

[151] John Locke, *Two Treatises of Government,* Ch. V Sec. 28 (1698) *available at* http://history.hanover.edu/early/locke/j-l2-007.htm.

[152] Nizan, P. et Duret, J. (eds.) *Karl Marx, Morceaux Choisis*, p. 263. Paris: Librairie Gallimard, (1934), (citing Karl Marx *Salaires, Prix et Profit*). Marx and Locke also agree on the distinction between use value and exchange value: http://lexnet.bravepages.com/LOCKE.htm-ftnref8. John Locke, *Of Civil Government*, Book II, Ch. V §46-51 eps. §50 id.; Karl Marx, *Contribution à la Critique de L'Economie Politique*, Paris, Editions Sociales; Karl Marx *Capitale*, Paris: Presses Universitaires Français (1993) p. 40.

[153] *See,* e.g., Murray N. Rothbard, ed., *The Logic of Action One*. (Edward Elgar Publishing Limited, 1997) pp.78-99.

[154] See, e.g., Ludwig Mises, *Money, Method and the Market Process,* Ch. 3, "Epistemological Relativism in the Sciences of Human Action" in Richard M. Ebeling. (ed.) Amsterdam: Kluwer Academic Publishers, 1990. (Article first published in 1962). Available at: http://www.mises.org/mmmp/mmmp3.asp.

[155] Hobbes' natural law (the law of the jungle) is clearly atomist. "The right of nature, which writers commonly call *jus naturale*, is the liberty each man hath to use his own power as he will himself for the preservation of his own nature; that is to say, of his own life; and consequently, of doing anything which, in his own judgement and reason, he shall conceive to be the aptest means thereunto." According to Hobbes, in the state of nature "right" is equivalent to "power" irrespective of society or family. Thomas Hobbes, *Leviathan* (1660), Chapter XIV, "Of The First And Second Natural Laws, And Of Contracts". *Available at:* http://www.uoregon.edu/~rbear/hobbes/leviathan.html.

[156] Only in so far as the *pacte sociale* constitutes society out of individuals adhesion to the supposed contract. This is however contradicts Rousseau's recognition that all states arise out of extended families. Jean-Jacques Rousseau, *Du Pacte Social*, Chapitre VI - Du Pacte Social; Chapitre II: Des premières sociétés, respectively (1762).

ty is now a product, not a relation.[157] However for Aristotle[158] and Rousseau[159] the autonomous, autarchic and thus independent human of the social contract postulated by Hobbes,[160] and Locke, in any of the various shades of that theory, is simply impossible.[161]

Though the social contract is not a historical fact and the state of nature an impossible fiction,[162] social contract theory appears to have influenced realist state theory, which sees the state as self sufficient but living in the state of nature as to other states,[163] and as such having only

---

[157] John Locke, *Two Treatises of Government*, "Of Property" Ch. V, Sec. 28 (1764) *available at:* http://history.hanover.edu/early/locke/j-l2-007.htm supra note 316.

[158] "He who thus considers things in their first growth and origin, whether a state or anything else, will obtain the clearest view of them. In the first place there must be a union of those who cannot exist without each other; namely, of male and female.... The family is the association established by nature for the supply of men's everyday wants... But when several families are united, and the association aims at something more than the supply of daily needs, the first society to be formed is the village.... When several villages are united in a single complete community, large enough to be nearly or quite self-sufficing, the state comes into existence, originating in the bare needs of life, and continuing in existence for the sake of a good life." Aristotle, *Politics* (translator: Benjamin Jowett) Book I, Part II, ca. 350 B.C.

[159] " La plus ancienne de toutes les sociétés et la seule naturelle est celle de la famille. » Jean-Jacques Rousseau, *Du Contrat Social ou Principes du Droit Politique* (1762) Livre I, Ch. II: Des premières sociétés, *available at:* http://un2sg4.unige.ch/athena/rousseau/jjr_cont.html.

[160] "the condition of man (as hath been declared in the precedent chapter) is a condition of war of every one against every one, in which case every one is governed by his own reason, and there is nothing he can make use of that may not be a help unto him in preserving his life against his enemies" Thomas Hobbes, *Leviathan*, Ch. XIV, Para. 4 (1660) *available at:* http://oregonstate.edu/instruct/phl302/texts/hobbes/leviathan-contents.html (searchable).

[161] "The philosophers, who have examined the foundations of society, have, every one of them, perceived the necessity of tracing it back to a state of nature, but not one of them has ever arrived there." Jean Jacques Rousseau (1712–1778). *On the Inequality among Mankind.* The Harvard Classics. 1909–14. *Available at:* http://www.bartleby.com/34/3/1002.html. *See also:* Jiri Priban, "Stealing the Natural Language: The Function of the Social Contract and Legality in the Light of Nietzche's Philosophy," 24 *Cardozo L.Rev.* 663, 664 (2003) *available at:* http://www.cardozo.yu.edu/cardlrev/v24n2/Priban%20Final%20Version.pdf.

[162] See, e.g. John Locke, Two Treatises of Government Ch. II "Of the State of Nature" (1764) *available at:* http://history.hanover.edu/early/locke/j-l2-004.htm.

[163] Kenneth N. Waltz, *Man, the State, and War* (1954).

one law, the law of the strongest. This is every bit as unrealistic as the social contract theory which appears to have spawned it and, like social contract theory, must be rejected because it too does not correspond to material reality. Social contract theory and realist state theory do not even have much heuristic utility for the presumptions of these theories are so contrary to actual fact that they cannot provide even an approximate or simplified view of how states are actually formed or actually behave.[164]

A credible argument can be made that in pursuing the autarchic individualist ideal of the enlightenment western society sowed the seeds of its own deracination and alienation, as Marx noted.[165] Still, though there are very real points of divergence, even within western theories of rights, the fact is both west and east see human rights as consequence of rationality and as implying or even being grounded upon social duties. Consequently, they can serve a key role in the post-Westphalian world.

Western theory does not ignore legal duties in practice. For example, the first part of the state constitution of the Free Hansa State Bremen is entitled "Fundamental rights and duties." [166] We can also see this in the East German Constitution which granted both a right and duty to work.[167]Again, in the Swiss Federal Constitution we see the duties are

---

[164] The simplified model of the economy provided by the "homo economicus" does, roughly, approximate how economic actors in fact behave. Like the states in IR realism, economic actors are posited as rational maximisers of their utility. However the economic game is positive sum, whereas IR theory generally proposes that IR is a zero sum game. In economic theory altruists can be safely ignored as they are a distinct minority. Realist IR assumptions do not in fact reduce the variables which influence state behavior in a meaningful way because the variables eliminated (economic factors) are more relevant than the ones retained (military factors)!

[165] Karl Marx, *Economic and Philosophic Manuscripts of 1844*, "The Alienation of Labor" (1844). Available at http://www.wsu.edu:8080/~dee/MODERN/ALIEN.HTM.

[166] Landesverfassung der Freien Hansestadt Bremen, Artikel 1 - 20, Erster Hauptteil: Grundrechte und Grundpflichten *available at:* http://www.bremen.de/info/skp/lv/Vrfssng1.htm.

[167] Verfassung der DDR, Artikel 24 *available at:* http://www.ddr-imwww.de/Gesetze/Verfassung.htm

"(1) Jeder Bürger der Deutschen Demokratischen Republik hat das Recht auf Arbeit. Er hat das Recht auf einen Arbeitsplatz und dessen freie Wahl entsprechend den gesellschaftlichen Erfordernissen und der persönlichen Qualifikation. Er hat das Recht auf Lohn nach Qualität und Quantität der Arbeit. Mann und Frau, Erwachsene und

also underlined.[168] This is not limited to the German speaking world. The French constitution also speaks of rights and duties as concomitant.[169]

2. Moral Relativism and Cultural Imperialism versus Universalism[170]

One attack on human rights argues that they are not universal,[171] either because no universal values exist (postmodernism)[172] or because human rights represent western values[173] (cultural relativism).[174]Both

---

Jugendliche haben das Recht auf gleichen Lohn bei gleicher Arbeitsleistung.

(2) Gesellschaftlich nützliche Tätigkeit ist eine ehrenvolle Pflicht für jeden arbeitsfähigen Bürger. Das Recht auf Arbeit und die Pflicht zur Arbeit bilden eine Einheit."

168 Schweizerische Bundesverfassung, Art. 6 Individuelle und gesellschaftliche Verantwortung

"Jede Person nimmt Verantwortung für sich selber wahr und trägt nach ihren Kräften zur Bewältigung der Aufgaben in Staat und Gesellschaft bei." *available at:* http://www.admin.ch/ch/d/sr/101/a6.html.

169 *Déclaration Des Droits De L'homme Et Du Citoyen De 1789* « Les Représentants du Peuple Français, constitués en Assemblée Nationale, considérant que l'ignorance, l'oubli ou le mépris des Droits de l'Homme sont les seules causes des malheurs publics et de la corruption des Gouvernements, ont résolu d'exposer, dans une Déclaration solennelle, les droits naturels, inaliénables et sacrés de l'Homme, afin que cette Déclaration, constamment présente à tous les Membres du corps social, leur rappelle sans cesse leurs droits et leurs devoirs » *available at:* http://www.assemblee-nat.fr/connaissance/constitution.asp.

170 Guyora Binder, "Cultural Relativism And Cultural Imperialism In Human Rights Law," 5 *Buff. Hum. Rts. L. Rev.* 211, 221 (1999) (Describes the universalism/relativism debate). Makau Mutua, "Savages, Victims, And Saviors: The Metaphor Of Human Rights," 42 *Harv. Int'l L.J.* 201, 204 (2001) (Points out the irony of brutalizing colonial powers pushing for the Nuremberg trials and adopting the UDHR).

171 For a discussion of the contours (and limits) of the universality/relativism debate in an intercultural comparative context *see:* Yash Ghai, *Universalism and Relativism: Human Rights as a Framework for Negotiating Interethnic Claims,* 21 Cardozo L.R. 1095 (2000) *available at:* http://www.undp.org.fj/elections/reports/ghai.pdf.

172 See, e.g., Zühtü Arslan, "Taking Rights Less Seriously: Postmodernism and Human Rights," 5 *Res Publica,* 195 *available at:* http://www.philosophy.ru/library/pdf/234617.pdf.

173 Richard Klein, "Cultural Relativism, Economic Development And International Human Rights In The Asian Context," 9 *Touro Int'l L. Rev.* 1 to 9 *Touro Int'l L. Rev.* 1, 4 (2001) (UDHR rooted in western values) supra note 226.

174Antonio Cassese *supra* note 2 at 52; Sarah Joseph, "A Rights Analysis Of The Covenant On Civil And Political Rights," 5 *J. Int'l Legal Stud.* 57 to 5 *J. Int'l Legal Stud.*

these attacks are erroneous.[175]

As we saw in the question of whether duties are *a priori* rights, the question of whether human rights is a universal concept can be posited in terms of a geographic schism between the industrialized north and the developing south.[176] Very different challenges to the universality of human rights arise in each of these regions due to differing economic conditions. However, neither challenge alone or in combination is sufficiently strong to defeat the theory that there are universally common characteristics of human nature, which in turn are the foundation of a similarly universal theory of human rights, which in turn engenders a legally binding practice of human rights.

These challenges are the result of cultural relativism in the north and accusations or fears of accusations of cultural imperialism by the south.[177] Not unsurprisingly the moral relativists are essentially westerners.[178] Neo-liberals such as Posner believe that there are no moral values and that there are only market values.[179] This is one of the splits between classical liberalism and neo-liberalism.

57, 74-75 (1999) (arguing that the distinction between rights and duties is artificial).

[175] "the cultural relativist theories of the academy are tautological and overly deterministic because they fail to appreciate the roles of both human agency and institutions in the transformative processes of cultural discourse." Michael C. Davis, *supra* note 138 at 110.

[176] See, e.g. Dianne Otto, *supra* note 363 at 1.

[177] Makau Mutua *Savages, Victims, And Saviors*, *supra* note 194 at 204-205 (Argues that human rights is eurocentric though well meaning and unknowingly reiterates colonial paradigms) *supra* note 336. And see, e.g., Jonathan C. Goltzman *Cultural Relativism or Cultural Intrusion? Female Ritual Slavery in Western Africa & the International Covenant on Civil and Political Rights: Ghana as a Case Study,* 4 N.Eng. Int'l & Comp. L. Ann. 53, 66 (1998) *available at:* http://www.nesl.edu/intljournal/vol4indx.cfm.

[178] For a good explanation of the problems of moral relativism (which however fails to recognize the fact that in any formal system axioms are necessary to formal representation and necessarily tautological) *see:* Michael J. Perry, "Moral Knowledge, Moral Reasoning, Moral Relativism: A 'Naturalist' Perspective," 20 *Ga. L. Rev.* 995, 1003-1009. (1986). (Proposing a method for valid normative inference using practical reasoning i.e. phronesis but discussing although only obliquely Hume's position on normative inference). A reply to moral relativism points out that for liberals like Rawls, Ackerman, and Dworkin there is no moral knowledge. Michael J. Perry, id. *at* 995 (1986). Aristotle and Locke believe in objective moral knowledge. Perry is identifying the neo-liberal (i.e. ultra-capitalist) abuse of the idea of liberality.

[179] See, e.g., Richard Posner, *The Economics of Justice* Boston: Harvard (1981).

The West seems to have a monopoly on moral relativism because of economics: westerners are products of societies of such superabundance that they can afford the luxury of entertaining ideas such as "all truths are relative."[180] Of course, if truth were only relative then no objective truth could exist. That however creates a paradox. A truth statement that no truth statements exist is itself a truth statement. Relativist arguments, whether as to epistemology, i.e. truth scepticism, or axiology, i.e. moral relativism, can be seen either as the product of confused reasoning[181] or a culture so blinded by its own wealth that it cannot see the starvation and death that are all too common in the third world.[182]

Because moral relativists often suffer from having never been con-

---

[180] The failure of the moral relativists to grasp reality can be shown by a crude reductio: genital mutilation. Who cares to argue for it? There is no absence of literature. See, e.g. Adam Karp, "Genitorts In The Global Context: Female Genital Mutilation As Tort Under The Alien Tort Claims Act, The Torture Victim Protection Act, And The Foreign Sovereign Immunities Act," 18 Women's Rts. L. Rep. 315 (1997); Sylvia Wynter "'Genital Mutilation' Or 'Symbolic Birth?' Female Circumcision, Lost Origins, And The Aculturalism Of Feminist/Western Thought," 47 Case W. Res. L. Rev. 501, 501 (1997); L. Amede Obiora, "Bridges And Barricades: Rethinking Polemics And Intransigence In The Campaign Against Female Circumcision," 47 Case W. Res. L. Rev. 275, 275 (1997). A moral relativist cannot oppose genital mutilation (or any other act) since all cultures are (to the relativist) equally valid. Epistemologically, truth scepticism must be distinguished from post-modernist truth abnegationism. Truth scepticism with roots in Nietzsche merely challenges whether what we are told is "truth" is in fact "true". Friedrich Nietzsche, Jenseits von Gut und Böse, (1887) available at: http://www.gutenberg2000.de/nietzsch/jenseits/0htmldir.htm. Truth abnegation denies the existence of truth.

[181] Much of the confusion lies in the belief that statements must be either true or false. Aristotle himself noted that some statements, such as prayers, have no truth value. "Every sentence has meaning, not as being the natural means by which a physical faculty is realized, but, as we have said, by convention. Yet every sentence is not a proposition; only such are propositions as have in them either truth or falsity. Thus a prayer is a sentence, but is neither true nor false." Aristotle, *On Interpretation* (c. 350 B.C.) (Translated by E. M. Edghill) Section 1, Part IV, para. 2 *Available at:* http://classics.mit.edu/Aristotle/interpretation.1.1.html. *Also see:* Sanford Shieh, "Undecidability, Epistemology, and Anti-Realist Intuitionism", 2 *Nordic Journal of Philosophical Logic* 55 available at: http://www.hf.uio.no/filosofi/njpl/vol2no2/decidable/decidable.pdf. One root of the confusion is the recognition by Kurt Gödel that the truth value of some propositions of formal logic cannot be determined by a formal system. Kurt Gödel, *On formally undecidable propositions of Principia Mathematica and related systems*, (1931) *available at:*

http://nago.cs.colourado.edu/~hirzel/papers/canon00-goedel.pdf.

[182] The best attacks on the universality of human rights focus on the cultural flaws of the north and question its moral legitimacy. E.g. "The human rights movement is marked

fronted with genuine moral choices, let alone a genuine moral dilemma, they threaten the very idea of rights which generated the abundance that they consume.[183] One might consider this, like most errors, to be a self correcting problem. However, due to the economic plight of the third world self correction is not the best correction in this case. Further, the mirror image in the third world, an accusation that the human rights discourse of the west is cultural imperialism,[184] is probably not self correcting. Thus a coherent defence of the universality of human rights is crucial if human rights are to serve as a key feature in the post-Westphalian world.

Given the west's history of attempts at "civilising" the third world[185]—labour exploitation in the colonial world was justified in the name of the Christian duty to "civilize" "savages"[186]—the wariness or skepticism[187] of the third world intellectual toward the conflation of western human rights with universal human rights[188] and the critique that human rights are a smokescreen for imperialism is understand-

---

by a damning metaphor. The grand narrative of human rights contains a subtext that depicts an epochal contest pitting savages, on the one hand, against victims and saviors, on the other." Makau Mutua, *supra* note 194 *at* 201. But even the best attacks criticise not the idea of human rights as such, but rather the legitimacy of the north/west to claim to be the fountain of human rights.

[183] "According to the naturalist conception, moral knowledge is knowledge of how to live so as to flourish, to achieve well-being." Michael J. Perry, *supra* note 345 at 997. Those who lack moral knowledge literally suffer from their ignorance, as Aristotle notes.

[184] Surya P. Subedi, "Are The Principles Of Human Rights "Western" Ideas? An Analysis Of The Claim Of The "Asian" Concept Of Human Rights From The Perspectives Of Hinduism," 30 *Cal. W. Int'l L.J.* 45, 45 (1999) (Arguing that the idea that human rights is the product of Western Christian civilization is reiteration of selective nineteenth-century values).

[185] Literally: imposing the civil law. Gabe S. Varges, *The New International Economic Order Legal Debate,* 1 (1983).

[186] Makau Mutua, "What is TWAIL?" 94 *ASIL Proceedings*, vol. 94, 1, 37. (2000).

[187] Surya P. Subedi, id. at 46. However once again that is not a dispute as to whether there are human rights but rather what is the content of those rights. As such it is no argument against the universality of human rights.

[188] For example, Nestlé sells powdered milk in the third world erroneously arguing that it will make babies more intelligent then mother's milk. Further powdered milk requires sterilised water — and the water in the third world is often impure. Worse, powdered milk

able.[189] But, despite historical and economic distortion a basic fact of humanity is true: all healthy humans are rational and seek to enjoy the good life in society.[190] Moreover that rationality is precisely the foundation of fundamental rights. We have rights both because we are rational and because structures of rights allow us to use our rationality practically in order not only to survive and but also to attain the good life.[191] Were Europe a victim of Indian imperialism and Africa overfed and under worked we would see Europe expressing fears of cultural imperialism and India preaching some variety of moral relativism.[192] Rights are to a certain extent defined by a society's level of economic development.[193] Relatively impoverished pre-industrial or nascent industrial states simply cannot afford to impose affirmative claims posited by second generation rights. But that does not change the fact that the ultimate foundation and vector of rights is our inherent value as rational social beings.[194]

---

is often diluted leading to malnutrition and even death from starvation. When Nestlé was criticised for this in print Nestlé sued for defamation, specifically for *Verleumdung* and *üble Nachrede*. Nestlé's claim for *üble Nachrede* was upheld. Antonio Cassese *supra* note 2 *at* 138-139.

[189] "not all human rights principles have their roots in Western civilization nor are all human rights principles necessarily mere Western principles." Surya P. Subedi, *supra* note 354 at 45 (1999).

[190] Martha Minow, "Rights and Cultural Difference" in Sarat and Kearns *supra* note 147 at 355.

(example of human rights used as tool of domination of First Nations in North America). *Supra* note 139.

[190] See Aristotle, *Politics*, Book I Part II (Translated by Benjamin Jowett) (350 B.C.) *available at:* http://classics.mit.edu/Aristotle/politics.1.one.html.

[191] The good life is of course defined by Aristotle as the end of life in political society. *Id.*.

[192] In fact Indian discourses on human rights are well developed and even represented within western legal scholarship. See, e.g. Prakash Shah, "International Human Rights: A Perspective From India," 21 *Fordham Int'l L.J.* 24, 44 (1997).

[193] Yash Ghai, "Universalism And Relativism: Human Rights As A Framework For Negotiating Interethnic Claims" 21 *Cardozo L. Rev.* 1094, 1097 (2000) *available at:* http://www.cardozo.yu.edu/cardlrev/v21n4/ghai.pdf (citing to Chinese legal authority).

[194] Anita Ramasastry, "Corporate Complicity: From Nuremberg To Rangoon An Examination Of Forced Labor Cases And Their Impact On The Liability Of Multinational Corporations," 20 *Berkeley J. Int'l L.* 91, 153 (2002).

3. Human Rights and the rule of law?

Human rights as legal rules cannot exist without a society based on the rule of law.[195] The rule of law is not a uniquely westernconcept:[196] Asian societies also observed and observe the formal requirements of the rule of law and in some cases have also achieved the positive goals of guaranteeing substantive human rights necessary to obtain the good life. Separation of powers and the right to rebel are western inputs to the stock of human knowledge but those are not defining characteristics of the rule of law.[197] The rule of law is a logical precondition to human rights.[198] Though the rule of law is a necessary precondition to human rights it is not also a sufficient condition;[199] it is a necessary and suffi-

---

[195] Robin West, *supra* note 271 at 259 (Equality the foundation of mutual respect).

[196] One can of course question whether the United States are committed to the rule of law: "the United States has deployed military forces in Grenada, Libya, Nicaragua, Panama, and Yugoslavia without authorization from the United Nations Security Council, as required by the U.N. Charter. The United States quit UNESCO, failed to pay its U.N. dues in a timely manner, withdrew from the jurisdiction of the International Court of Justice, and refused to comply with the International Court's orders on at least three occasions... the United States has repeatedly executed foreign nationals without according them the basic right to consult with their consular representatives... the United States has failed to ratify the International Convenant on Economic, Social and Cultural Rights, the American Convention on Human Rights, the Convention on the Elimination of All Forms of Discrimination Against Women, the Convention on the Rights of the Child, and the Convention on the Prohibition of the Use, Stockpiling, Production and Transfer of Anti-Personnel Mines. ... the Bush administration rejected the Kyoto Protocol on global warming, the Comprehensive Nuclear Test Ban Treaty, the Biological Weapons Protocol to enforce the 1972 Convention on the Prohibition of the Development, Production, and Stockpiling of Bacteriological (Biological) and Toxin Weapons, which banned such weapons, and the Rome Statute of the International Criminal Court." Joel R. Paul, *supra* note 132 at 287-288.

[197] Charles Montesquieu, *De L'Esprit des Lois* (1758), Livre XI, *available at:* http://www.uqac.uquebec.ca/zone30/Classiques_des_sciences_sociales/livres/montesquieu/montesquieu.html. "the American and French Revolutions... established the right of the people to rebel against tyranny." Nancy P. Kelly, "The Political Offense Exemption To Extradition: Protecting The Right Of Rebellion In An Era Of International Political Violence," 66 *Or. L. Rev.* 405, 405 (1987). Though Hobbes and Rousseau consider the social contract irrevocable this is not Locke's position. John Locke, *Two Treatises of Government*, Ch. XIX §22 (1764) *available at* http://history.hanover.edu/early/locke/j-l2-001.htm.

[198] Report of the Joseph R. Crowley Program, "One Country, Two Legal Systems?" 23 *Fordham Int'l L.J.* 1, 6 (1999).

[199] Similarly, there is also no necessary connection between democracy and the rule of

cient condition of a market economy.[200] The rule of law ultimately can lead to human rights because the rule of law creates necessary pre-conditions for economic prosperity.[201]

How does a society which guarantees and achieves substantive human rights outcomes emerge from a conception of the rule of law as merely formal procedures?[202] Human rights emerge from the miasma of postmodern moral relativism and greed because they assert the truly universal aspects of humanity—rationality and essential dignity.[203] As a consequence of our rationality we have the capacity to acquire and alienate. Our rational nature separates us from other animals and is also the foundation of our essential dignity. Thus, certain rights are inalienable.[204]

---

law. Michel Rosenfeld, "The Rule Of Law And The Legitimacy Of Constitutional Democracy," 74 *S. Cal. L. Rev.* 1307, 1308 (2001).

[200] Richard L. Abel, "Capitalism and the Rule of Law: Precondition or Contradiction?" 28 *Law & Soc'y Rev.* 971, 987 (journal renamed: was 15 *Law & Social Inquiry* 685) (1990).

[201] "Human Rights ensure international security and prosperity" Speech by the Foreign Secretary, Jack Straw, to the United Nations Commission on Human Rights, Geneva, 17 April 2002 *available at:*
http://www.britischebotschaft.de/en/news/items/020418.htm.

[202] One possible answer is for realist reasons, i.e. *Realpolitik* considerations. The rule of law, like human rights, can be a tool in a state's diplomatic arsenal and serve its foreign policy goals. José Maravall, *The Rule of Law as a Political Weapon*, Working Paper 2001/160 (2001) *available at:* http://www.march.es/NUEVO/IJM/CEACS/PUBLICACIONES/WORKING%20PAPERS/2001_160.pdf.

[203] For good critiques of the flaws and confusion which inherent in postmodern thought due to an erroneous axiology and epistemology *see:* Dennis W. Arrow, "Pomobabble: Postmodern Newspeak and Constitutional 'Meaning' for the Uninitiated," 96 *Mich.L.R.* 461 (1997); Dennis Arrow, "Spaceball (Or, Not Everything that's Left is Postmodern)," 54 *Vand. L. Rev.* 2381 *available at:* http://law.vanderbilt.edu/lawreview/vol546/arrow.pdf.

[204] Aristotle argues that man outside of political society is rendered beastlike. "The proof that the state is a creation of nature and prior to the individual is that the individual, when isolated, is not self-sufficing; and therefore he is like a part in relation to the whole. But he who is unable to live in society, or who has no need because he is sufficient for himself, must be either a beast or a god: he is no part of a state." Aristotle, *Politics*, Book I, Part II (ca. 350 B.C.) *available at:* http://classics.mit.edu/Aristotle/politics.1.one.html.

C. THE GENERATIONAL THEORY OF HUMAN RIGHTS

The growth of human rights has roughly paralleled economic development, and is usually described as having evolved over time in three successive waves[205] from easily implemented individual negative claims to freedom from the state to positive collective claims to entitlements to state resources.[206] At least one scholar has tried to draw an ahistorical but philosophically interesting parallel between first generation rights as expressions of liberty, second generation rights as expressions of equality, and third generation rights as expressions of solidarity.[207] Such a description is almost poetic in its symmetry: and clearly the Declaration des Droits de l'Homme de 1789[208] did inspire the Universal

---

[205] But *see:* Dianne Otto, "Rethinking The "Universality" Of Human Rights Law," 29 *Colum. Hum. Rts. L. Rev.* 1 to 29 *Colum. Hum. Rts. L. Rev.* 1, 5-6 (1997). (Describing human rights as having developed in four generations — Otto's view is distinctly the minority view; Otto also describes the usual typology of first generation and second generation rights but subdivides third generation rights based on whether they arose out of the Soviet Bloc or Non-Aligned Movement). Claire Moore Dickerson, "Human Rights: The Emerging Norm Of Corporate Social Responsibility," 76 *Tul. L. Rev.* 1431 to 76 *Tul. L. Rev.* 1431, 1441-1442 (2002) (Describes and refines the three generation theory of human rights).

[206] John King Gamble, Teresa A. Bailey, Jared S. Hawk, Erin E. McCurdy, *supra* note 116 *at* 36 (Argues that first generation rights are able to be easily and immediately implemented). But *see* Claire Moore Dickerson, *supra* note 169 *at* 1444. Dickerson's ignores the individualist propertarian presumptions of first generation rights practice and claims of rights to collective bargaining which were raised only with the second generation of rights. John King Gamble, Teresa A. Bailey, Jared S. Hawk, Erin E. McCurdy, *supra* note 116 *at* 36 (2001). Jennifer A. Downs, *supra* note 209 *at* 351 (Argues that the generational theory is metaphoric not historic).

[207] "The first generation of political and civil rights, embodied in the Universal Declaration and the Covenant on Civil and Political Rights, are freedoms from state intrusion: liberté. The second generation furthers realization of the first generation by guaranteeing minimum standards, demandable upon the state, of education and health, a liveable wage, decent working conditions, and social insurance for all persons: egalite. Finally, the third generation consists of rights which may be invoked against and demanded of the state. These rights require all the organs of society — individual, state, regional, and international — to cooperate in order for the rights to be realised: fraternité." Jennifer A. Downs, "A Healthy And Ecologically Balanced Environment: An Argument For A Third Generation Right" 3 *Duke J. Comp. & Int'l L.* 351, 364 (1993). Supra note 209 at 364. I have found no evidence for this assertion in the writings of Diderot, Montesqieu or Rousseau.

[208] Déclaration des droits de l'Homme et du citoyen 26 août 1789 *available at:* http://www.justice.gouv.fr/textfond/ddhc.htm.

Declaration of Human Rights (UDHR).[209] However, the idea of three waves of rights did not spring like Athena fully formed from the mind of Zeus in 1789.[210] Louis Sohn traces the concept of three generations of human rights to Karel Vasak of UNESCO, whom Sohn quotes as the source of the term.[211] Sohn, quoting Vasek, believes that each generation of rights complements and completes the other. Sohn points out that Vasek linked the idea of generational rights to the motto of the French revolution—liberté, égalité, fraternité. But nothing in the writings of Montesquieu or Rousseau, or even Locke, Hobbes, or Kant[212] supports the theory that human rights would unfold in successive generations.[213] The idea seems to be a neologism,[214] an historical observation *ex post* and not a theoretical framework *ex ante*. A better typology might justify the generational split not on the basis of history or teleology but rather on positive international law. First generation international human rights appear to be a part of *jus cogens*.[215] Second generation rights are also customary laws but may be derogated from. Third generation rights are aspirational goals.

---

[209] Die Allgemeine Erklärung der Menschenrechte, Resolution 217 A (III) vom 10.12.1948, *available at:* http://www.unhchr.ch/udhr/lang/ger.htm.

[210] Anonymous, *Athena* (2002) http://www.mythologica.de/athena.htm.

[211] Louis B. Sohn, *supra* note 5 at 61-62.

[212] Charles Montesquieu, *L'Esprit des Lois* (1758) *available at:* http://www.uqac.uquebec.ca/zone30/Classiques_des_sciences_sociales/livres/montesquieu/de_esprit_des_lois/de_esprit_des_lois_tdm.html. *Le Contrat Social supra* note 172. *Two Treatises of Government*, supra note 174. *Leviathan*, supra note 20. Immanuel Kant, *Zum ewigen Frieden* (1795) *available at:* http://www.mda.de/homes/matban/de/kant-zef.html; Immanuel Kant, *Beantwortung der Frage: Was ist Aufklärung?* (1784). Available at: http://www.gutenberg2000.de/kant/aufklae/aufkl001.htm.

[213] I am of course open to contradiction and do not claim to have read the entire canon of every western enlightenment thinker. However it seems unlikely that the enlightenment thinkers foresaw with such clarity the future development of human rights.

[214] Louis B. Sohn, *supra* note 5 at 61-62.

[215] Louis B. Sohn, *id.* at 32.

1. First Generation Rights

The first wave of human rights in modernity is usually identified with the Scottish enlightenment[216] and the age of reason (XIXth century) expressed in the liberal revolutions[217] in America, France, and Latin America.[218] Rights asserted in these revolutions were essentially claims of the individual against state interference and to self government. That is the first generation rights (e.g., the freedom to worship, to peaceably assemble) were negative restrictions on state power.[219] First generation rights also tend to be procedural rights, rules which determine the creation or application of substantive claims to material goods.[220] Another common characteristic of first generation of rights is that historically they tend to see property rights as fundamental, individual and even

---

[216] R. Randall Kelso, "A Post-Conference Reflection On Federalism, Toleration, And Human Rights," 40 *S. Tex. L. Rev.* 811, 826-827 (two historical strands to moral reasoning about universal human rights: the Enlightenment natural law tradition, and the classic and Christian natural law tradition).

[217] Id; Louis B. Sohn, *supra* note 5 *at* 33. Kelso seems to ignore contemporary theorists of *ius naturale* such as Finnis.

[218] Because of this bourgeois influence on the idea of human rights some are skeptical as to whether human rights truly "liberates". This skepticism is understandable. Indeed as such critics of human rights note, rights are not merely a protection of the weak and innocent against the strong and powerful, they are also a vector of state power, and a subtle one at that. See, e.g. Wendy Brown, "Rights and Identity in Late Modernity," in Sarat and Kearns *supra* note *147 at* 89.

[219] U.S. Constitution, Amendments I (freedom of speech, worship) IV, (no unlawful search or seizure) *inter alia available at:* http://www.law.cornell.edu/constitution/constitution.billofrights.htm.

[220] *Id., e.g.* U.S. Constitution, Amendment V, *available at* http://www.law.cornell.edu/constitution/constitution.billofrights.htm and Déclaration des droits de l'Homme et Citoyen Articles 7-9 : supra note 159. « Article 7 - Nul homme ne peut être accusé, arrêté ou détenu que dans les cas déterminés par la loi et selon les formes qu'elle a prescrites. Ceux qui sollicitent, expédient, exécutent ou font exécuter des ordres arbitraires doivent être punis ; mais tout citoyen appelé ou saisi en vertu de la loi doit obéir à l'instant ; il se rend coupable par la résistance. Article 8 - La loi ne doit établir que des peines strictement et évidemment nécessaires,et nul ne peut être puni qu'en vertu d'une loi établie et promulguée antérieurement au délit, et légalement appliquée. Article 9 - Tout homme étant présumé innocent jusqu'à ce qu'il ait été déclaré coupable, s'il est jugé indispensable de l'arrêter, toute rigueur qui ne serait pas nécessaire pour s'assurer de sa personne doit être sévèrement réprimée par la loi.

available at : http://www.justice.gouv.fr/textfond/ddhc.htm.

absolute.[221] Later generations of rights see property as relative and socially conditioned.[222] First generation rights are, roughly, negative civil and political rights—"freedoms from" rather than "rights to." However, the right to worship as one chooses to write or speak one's mind are not mere restrictions on state power— they are also assertions of the individual's power.[223] Most restrictions of state power imply an exercise of individual power and vice-versa.

Rights discourse is inherently problematic because of this dual nature of rights and because "rights" are expressed as vague or ambiguous platitudes. Rights discourse is also contested because the interest of the individual and the collective are at times in conflict and one or the other must prevail and because of the classic duality of "substance" versus "procedure."[224] But though the usual account of the historical development of human rights is not perfectly accurate and though human rights are inherently problematic that does not mean that there is no common concept of an idea that humans have inherent rights and there is even some agreement as to at least a common core of universally recognized human rights such as the right not to be deprived arbitrarily of one's own life.

---

[221] Declaration des Droits de l'Homme et Citoyen, Art. 2, 17 *available at* : http://www.justice.gouv.fr/textfond/ddhc.htm ; U.S. Constitution, Amendment V *available at* : http://www.law.cornell.edu/constitution/constitution.billofrights.html#amendmentiii.

[222] E.g. "not every destruction or injury to property by governmental action has been held to be a 'taking' in the constitutional sense." *Armstrong v. United States*, 364 U.S. 40, 48 (1960).

[223] E.g. Declaration des Droits de l'Homme et Citoyen, art. 10 & 11:« Article 10 - Nul ne doit être inquiété pour ses opinions, mêmes religieuses, pourvu que leur manifestation ne trouble pas l'ordre public établi par la loi. Article 11 - La libre communication des pensées et des opinions est un des droits les plus précieux de l'homme ; tout citoyen peut donc parler, écrire, imprimer librement, sauf à répondre de l'abus de cette liberté dans les cas déterminés par la loi. *available at* : http://www.justice.gouv.fr/textfond/ddhc.htm. Clearly these are restrictions of the state's power— but they are often also affirmations of the individual's power.

[224] Paul W. Kahn, "American Hegemony And International Law Speaking Law To Power: Popular Sovereignty, Human Rights, And The New International Order," 1 *Chi. J. Int'l L.* 1, 5 (2000). (Points out the collapse of dualism and that sovereignty rather than a solution to the problems of peace and justice is a problem) supra note 50.

2. Second Generation Rights

The second generation of rights arose during the industrial revolution and was contemporaneous with the political revolutions of circa 1848-1870.[225] Human rights were then seen increasingly as no longer merely negative rights to freedom from state interference but rather as affirmative substantive[226] social claims to state resources.[227] Second generation rights were seen as the consequence of dialectical class struggle[228] and thus to some extent as collective rights.[229] Second generation rights discourse tends, unlike first generation rights analysis, to see property claims as social and relative.

---

[225] Louis B. Sohn *supra* note 5 at 33 (1982). Claire Moore Dickerson, *supra* note *169* at 76 *Tul. L. Rev.* 1431 to 76 *Tul. L. Rev.* 1431, 1444-1445 (2002) (Describes three generation rights theory).

[226] E.g., Verfassung der DDR, Artikel 25: "(1) Jeder Bürger der Deutschen Demokratischen Republik hat das gleiche Recht auf Bildung. Die Bildungsstätten stehen jedermann offen. Das einheitliche sozialistische Bildungssystem gewährleistet jedem Bürger eine kontinuierliche sozialistische Erziehung. Bildung und Weiterbildung." *Available at:* http://www.ddr-im-www.de/Gesetze/Verfassung.htm and *at:* http://www.documentarchiv.de/ddr/verfddr.html.

[227] E.g. Landesverfassung der Freien Hansestadt Bremen Artikel 14: "Jeder Bewohner der Freien Hansestadt Bremen hat Anspruch auf eine angemessene Wohnung. Es ist Aufgabe des Staates und der Gemeinden, die Verwirklichung dieses Anspruches zu fördern." *available at:* http://www.bremen.de/info/skp/lv/Vrfssng1.htm.

[228] Präambel, Verfassung der DDR, 6 April 1968: "In Fortsetzung der revolutionären Traditionen der deutschen Arbeiterklasse und gestützt auf die Befreiung vom Faschismus hat das Volk der Deutschen Demokratischen Republik in Übereinstimmung mit den Prozessen der geschichtlichen Entwicklung unserer Epoche sein Recht auf sozial-ökonomische, staatliche und nationale Selbstbestimmung verwirklicht und gestaltet die entwickelte sozialistische Gesellschaft." *Available at: Available at:* http://www.ddr-im-www.de/Gesetze/Verfassung.htm#sozgesell.

[229] Landesverfassung der Freien Hansestadt Bremen vom 21. Oktober 1947 (Brem.GBl. S. 251) "Erschüttert von der Vernichtung, die die autoritäre Regierung der Nationalsozialisten unter Mißachtung der persönlichen Freiheit und der Würde des Menschen in der jahrhundertealten Freien Hansestadt Bremen verursacht hat, sind die Bürger dieses Landes willens, eine Ordnung des gesellschaftlichen Lebens zu schaffen, in der die soziale Gerechtigkeit, die Menschlichkeit und der Friede gepflegt werden, in der der wirtschaftlich Schwache vor Ausbeutung geschützt und allen Arbeitswilligen ein menschenwürdiges Dasein gesichert wird." Präambel, Landesverfassung Bremen, *available at:* http://www.bremen.de/info/skp/lv/Vrfssng1.htm A comparison of the preamble of the Bremer constitution and the preamble of the East German constitution reveals several interesting equivalences, paralells and divergences.

On this point there is some tension between the first and second generation rights.[230] For example, the social welfare and social insurance schemes of industrial states and social democracies are second generation rights—but those rights infringe on the property rights guaranteed by first generation rights.[231] However, while that is the case, the second generation rights also appease the dispossessed and as such tend to increase social stability. Thus second generation rights function ultimately to maintain property rights.

Not only is there surface tension between first and second generation rights on the issue of property rights, the usual evolutionary generational understanding of human rights is incomplete: are the rights of women a first generation procedural right or a second generation substantive right or a third generation collective right? Historically claims to women's rights only began to be made around 1880, which would place them in the second generation. But those claims were to procedural rights, such as the right to vote, or freedoms from state restrictions on employment and property ownership. So theoretically at least the early women's rights were first generation rights—but historically they were only recognized just after the rise of the second generation of human rights circa 1880. Proponents of the generational theory should explicitly declare their description of three generations of rights as either theoretical (the author's position) or historical in order to avoid misunderstanding and to clarify the points where history and theory diverge.

This is not the only example of historical contradiction within the

---

[230] Jennifer A. Downs, *supra* note 209 *at* 360-361 (Argues, in my opinion unconvincingly, that first and second generation rights live in symbiosis and are not in fact in conflict).

[231] E.g., Russian Constitution of 1936 Art. 120 (right to pensions for the elderly) *available at:* http://www.departments.bucknell.edu/russian/const/36cons04.html#chap10. Usually social insurance in the liberal democracies is a part of administrative law. Sometimes however it does enter into constitutional law. E.g., Art. 41 Bundesverfassung Schweiz: "1 Bund und Kantone setzen sich in Ergänzung zu persönlicher Verantwortung und privater Initiative dafür ein, dass: a. jede Person an der sozialen Sicherheit teilhat; ..." *available at:* http://www.admin.ch/ch/d/sr/101/a41.html C.f., Constitution Francaise, Art. 1 *available at:* http://www.assemblee-nat.fr/connaissance/constitution.asp. Constitution Française, 4 Octobre 1958, Article premier «La France est une République indivisible, laïque, démocratique et sociale. Elle assure l'égalité devant la loi de tous les citoyens sans distinction d'origine, de race ou de religion. Elle respecte toutes les croyances.

idea of human rights. What about the rights of non-whites? Emancipation of black persons occurred in the mid 19th century circa 1860.[232] This was another claim to freedom from state power—the right not to be property, the right to vote, the right to speak. Racial inequality was *de facto*, and sometimes *de jure* well into the 20th century in the U.S.[233] and even (with resistance) into the 1980s in South Africa.[234] The historical description of three generations of human rights must thus acknowledge two major incongruencies: the delay in recognizing womens' rights and the denial, at least until relatively recently, of the human rights of non-whites.

Although these instances of historical inconsistencies demonstrate the limits of the idea of a "first" wave of procedural negative rights and a "second" generation substantive affirmative claims, with these qualifications the usual historical account of the evolution of human rights can help us to understand why the revolutions of 1776 and 1789 wrought different changes than those of 1917[235] and 1949 provided we indicate whether we are speaking of the three generations theory as an abstract description, where it is roughly accurate (with qualification) or as a historical description, where it is only loosely accurate.[236]

---

[232] E.g., The Emancipation Proclamation, (1863) *avalable at.:* http://www.nps.gov/ncro/anti/emancipation.html.

[233] *Plessy V. Ferguson*, 163 U.S. 537 (1896) (segregated railways not unconstitutional later overruled), *available at:* http://afroamhistory.about.com/library/blplessy_v_ferguson.htm; *Cumming v. Board Of Ed. Of Richmond County*, 175 U.S. 528 (1899) (segregated education not unconstitutional, later overruled) *available at:* http://afroamhistory.about.com/library/blcumming_v_richmond.htm.

[234] For a listing of the principle apartheid legislation and history *see:* BBC, *The Story of Africa: Southern Africa* (2003) *at:* http://www.bbc.co.uk/worldservice/africa/features/storyofafrica/12chapter7.shtml.

[235] Louis B. Sohn, *supra* note 5 at 33.

[236] For a discussion of the role of revolution in international law (and as expression of the right of national self determination) see Theodor Schweisfurth, *The Role of Political Revolution in the Theory of International Law* in Macdonald & Johnston *supra* note 21 at 913.

3. Third Generation Rights

The third generation of human rights arose in the post-war world.[237] The recognition of third generation rights is sometimes also linked to the recognition of limited international legal personality.[238] Third generation rights are seen as essentially collective.[239] They seek to dynamically complement the rights of the first and second generation.[240] That attempt however is somewhat doomed from inception, because of the inherent tension between the individual/propertarian basis of first generation rights and the collective/social basis of second generation rights. Despite that fact, third generation rights are said to include the right to peace,[241] the right to security,[242] the right to democracy and the right to environmentally sustainable economic development.[243]

Is there anything in the third generation rights which makes them inherently collective? If so, does that inherent factor mean that individ-

---

[237] Jennifer A. Downs, *supra* note 209 at 362. (Cites Karel Vasak, Legal Adviser to the United Nations Educational, Scientific, and Cultural Organization (UNESCO) and former director of the UNESCO Division of Human Rights and Peace, as the first to use the term 'third generation human rights').

[238] "Comment, Developments In The Law — International Environmental Law: V. Institutional Arrangements," 104 *Harv. L. Rev.* 1580, 1600 (1991) (Notes that individuals have limited rights and duties under international human rights law).

[239] Claire Moore Dickerson, *supra* note 169 at 1445-1446 (Describes third generation rights as collective solidarity rights).

[240] Jennifer A. Downs, *supra* note 209 at 363 (third generation of rights a consequence of a dynamic view of human rights). And id. at 358 (1993) (describes generational theory of rights).

[241] Declaration on the Right of Peoples to Peace, G.A. res. 39/11, annex, 39 U.N. GAOR Supp. (No. 51) at 22, U.N. Doc. A/39/51 (1984). *Available at:* http://www1.umn.edu/humanrts/instree/q3drpp.htm.

[242] J. Oloka-Onyango, "Human Rights And Sustainable Development In Contemporary Africa: A New Dawn, Or Retreating Horizons?" 6 *Buff. Hum. Rts. L. Rev.* 39, 43 (2000) supra note 245.

[243] African Charter on Human and Peoples' Rights June, 26, 1981, O.A.U. Doc. CAB/LEG/67/3/Rev. 5, arts. 19-24 (entered into force Oct. 21, 1986), reprinted in 21 I.L.M. 58 (1982). 1986 Declaration on the Right to Development. Adopted by General Assembly resolution 41/128 of 4 December 1986 *available at*: http://193.194.138.190/html/menu3/b/74.htm Also see, e.g. Isabella D. Bunn, *The Right To Development: Implications For International Economic Law* 15 Am. U. Int'l L. Rev. 1425 to 15 Am. U. Int'l L. Rev. 1425, 1426 (2000) Arguing for "the emergence of the right to development."

uals should not have a cause of action? And if individuals have a claim for third generation rights, is not that claim then substantive? It is this author's opinion that while these rights are necessarily collective—peace, democracy, and development are not individual phenomena—the enforcement of these rights could be placed in the hands of individuals and linked to substantive material goods. In actual fact however the positive force of third generation collective rights is contestable, particularly since the fall of the Soviet system. Third generation rights are usually seen as hortatory goals which guide and direct the development of the law.

Because there is some tension between first and second generation rights and a lack of dialogue between third generation rights and earlier conceptions of rights and because of historical inexactitude, the usual typology of three generations of human rights is inaccurate but not so inaccurate that it must be rejected.[244] Instead the theory must, like most theories, be qualified and adapted to conform to reality. It is only where reality so fails to conform to a model's descriptions and predictions that that legal science (like any other science) must reject the model and formulate a new one. That is not the case of the historical account of the evolution of human rights through three stages. However the Westphalian theory of the state as absolute hermetic sovereign no longer corresponds to material reality. Modifying that model is probably impossible due to fundamental changes in technology, and even if the theory could be modified that may actually be undesirable if the Westphalian model of the state led the world to two global wars.

As we have seen the traditional analysis which sees human rights as evolving in three successive waves is only partially complete. It is true, very roughly, that conceptions of human rights have evolved from individual rights to collective claims. It is also true, theoretically, that we can distinguish between rights of the individual and of the collective

---

[244] The U.S. generally opposes the idea of a third generation of human rights in international law. But see Barbara Stark, "Economic Rights In The United States And International Human Rights Law: Toward An 'Entirely New Strategy'," 44 *Hastings L.J.* 79 to 44 *Hastings L.J.* 79, 130 (1992) suggesting that third generation rights in the U.S. are protected at the state level rather than the federal level. That view ignores that those claims are generally not defended as inalienable rights but rather are stated to be conditional entitlements accorded to individuals by the state as an act of largesse. A conditional entitlement must be distinguished from an inalienable right.

and freedoms from state interference and rights to state resources. However, the three generation analysis ignores certain cross currents and tensions between those rights and also other evolutionary developments which are not generally identified in rights discourse. As such it can only be used with these qualifications as a tool to describe contemporary reality.

a. Individual and Collective Rights

The typical description of human rights is somewhat problematic. If we shift our focus though we can better understand human rights. The generational perspective focuses on the content of the right, i.e. the character of the right. However it ignores who holds the right. Instead of asking "What right is held?" we will ask "Who holds the right?" When we ask the question "who holds the right?" a different view emerges. Having this different view is important because future rights discourse will probably be characterized by a struggle between western/universalist market rights (e.g., the WTO) and local, collective and possibly fundamentalist conceptions of collective rights.[245]

Just as the content of rights has evolved with historical development, conceptions of who is entitled to claim a right have also evolved. The conception of who is entitled to claim a right has evolved from an understanding of the holder of legal rights as the individual white male adult citizen to the holder of rights as including non-whites,[246] women, and ultimately non-citizens and children and finally collectives.[247] This progress in the ability to hold a right is basically ignored in the traditional generational view which focuses on what right is held rather than on who holds the right. This must be pointed out however in order to escape from the hierarchical and patriarchical origins of human rights seen in Aristotle's thought which leads to unjust inequalities.[248]

---

[245] See, e.g. Alan Greenspan, The Embrace of Free Markets, Remarks at the Woodrow Wilson Award Dinner of the Woodrow Wilson International Center for Scholars, New York, New York June 10, 1997.

[246] See, e.g. U.S. Constitution, Amdt. XIV. Supra note 402.

[247] Thus, radical critiques of human rights as a vector of power are not without foundation. See, e.g. Martha Minow, "Rights and Cultural Difference" in Sarat and Kearns *supra* note *139 at* 355.

[248] See e.g., Aristotle, *Politics,* Book I Part XIII. *Available at:* http://classics.mit.edu/

The idea of women's rights and rights against racial discrimination do not harmonize well with the generational perspective of rights. Neither women's rights nor the rights of non-white persons are claims to entitlement but both women and non-whites were ignored by individualist first generation rights theory. Perhaps this is because these rights though enjoyed by individuals are derived from collectives—and first generation rights are essentially individualistic. In any event, women were in fact only emancipated relatively late in history—in many cases only in the last century and in some cases women remain unemancipated, most obviously in the Islamic world but elsewhere as well.[249] Islamic scholars would point out that the right of a woman to seek divorce was first recognized by Islam, as was racial equality.[250] Islamic feminists would also argue that human rights include the right to be treated with dignity and respect and that dress codes enforce that respect and that equality of rights does not mean equal roles. This author views the historical argument as more persuasive. Islam clearly assigns specific roles based on gender. However the 'liberation' of women in the west should be questioned as this 'liberation' serves the interests of consumerism and capitalism. Western women may have traded the kitchen for the office—yet are still expected to maintain the kitchen.[251]

Aristotle/politics.mb.txt

supra note 164. Aristotle even recognizes that his arguments for natural slavery and the natural inequality of men and women are flawed, and tries to meet the objections. Aristotle, *id.,* Book I Part VI. *Available at:* http://classics.mit.edu/Aristotle/politics.mb.txt. Aristotle clearly believed that some people were inherently destined for slavery. *Id.*, Book One, Part v. *Available at:* http://classics.mit.edu/Aristotle/politics.mb.txt.

[249] But *see:* Joelle Entelis, "International Human Rights: Islam's Friend Or Foe?" 20 *Fordham Int'l L.J.* 1251, 1251 (1997). Arguing that Algeria is an Example of the Compatibility of International Human Rights law and Islamic law regarding women.

[250] E.g., Riffat Hassan, *Religious Human Rights In Global Perspective: Religious Perspectives* 361-86 (John Witte, Jr. and Johan D. van der Vyver eds., Martinus Nijhoff Publishers, 1996) *available at:* http://www.law.emory.edu/EILR/volumes/spring96/hassan.html.

[251] For a discussion of Islamic human rights law and international human rights law *see:* Bharathi Anandhi Venkatraman, "Islamic States And The United Nations Convention On The Elimination Of All Forms Of Discrimination Against Women: Are The Shari'a And The Convention Compatible?" 44 *Am. U. L. Rev.* 1949, 1951 (1995).

Likewise, apartheid was the norm at least until the 1950s—well after the beginning of the second generational social rights to substantive goods.[252] The rights of sexual dissidents, such as homosexuals and transvestites and transgendered persons remain essentially ignored throughout the world.[253] Some groups still must be protected.

b. Property Rights

Another tension between first and second generation rights often ignored by the usual generational perspective is the fact that while property rights played a central theoretical role in first generation rights discourse, as both the means and end of the good life,[254] and though, at least since the fall of the Soviet Union the practical importance of property rights has increased, their theoretical role has decreased. Today it is nearly universally admitted that reasonable restrictions on property rights are permissible.[255] This is an interesting fact because in terms of economic development there is no reason for it: perhaps the field of human rights is dominated by altruists just as the field of commercial law is dominated by practical businesslike persons? If there is legal interpretive flexibility in the future resolution of the dialectic between rights as economic negative limitations on government *versus* rights as positive expressions of local and indigenous sovereignty it may be found here.

Theoretically, the first generation of human rights was shaped by liberalism, exemplified in the writings of Rousseau, Locke and Kant though rooted much more deeply in the thought of Aristotle.[256] The sec-

---

[252] Population Registration Act 30 of 1950; Group Areas Act 41 of 1950; Separate Representation of Voters Act 45 of 1951 (Union of South Africa).

[253] *But see: Lawrence v. Texas*, 539 U.S. ___ (2003); *Dudgeon v. U.K.*, 45 Eur. Ct. H.R. (1981). And see, e.g., James D. Wilets, "International Human Rights Law And Sexual Orientation," 18 *Hastings Int'l & Comp. L. Rev.* 1 to 18 *Hastings Int'l & Comp. L. Rev.* 1, 1 (1994).

[254] Aristotle, *Nicomachean Ethics,* Book I § 2, (Translated by W.D. Ross)(350 B.C.) http://classics.mit.edu/Aristotle/nicomachaen.1.i.html.

[255] This is true even in the United States. See, e.g. *United States et al. v. Locke et al.* 471 U.S. 84;105 S. Ct. 1785; 85 L. Ed. 2d 64; 1985 U.S. LEXIS 197;53 U.S.L.W. 4433; 84 Oil & Gas Rep. 299 (1985).

[256] Jean-Jacques Rousseau, *Du Contrat Social Ou Principes Du Droit Politique* (1752) *available at* : http://www.google.de/search?q=rousseau+contrat+social&ie=ISO-8859-

ond and third generations of rights were in contrast influenced by Marx,[257] Engels, Lenin, and Mao. This raises an implicit question: what is the future of rights discourse now that the Soviet Union has collapsed?

Many theorists, particularly in the U.S., regard the end of the U.S.S.R. as a net gain for human rights.[258] This is however not exactly the case. Marxist human rights theory assigns survival rights such as food and shelter a higher value than property rights or the right to worship. So at least from that perspective gaining the right to worship freely and losing the right to a job would be seen as a net loss. Further, it is clear that the economic situation in Russia and the C.I.S. has deteriorated severely in the last 10 years with a resulting increase in crime and decline in human rights.[259] Similar regression has also occurred in South Africa. Formally, human rights are better protected there because of the

---

1&hl=de&meta=. John Locke, *Second Treatise on Government* (1690) *available at:* http://libertyonline.hypermall.com/Locke/second/second-frame.html. Epistemologically, Kant's *Kritik der reinen Vernunft* (1787) (*available at:* http://www.gutenberg2000.de/kant/krvb/krvb.htm) is the more important work, though in international law Kant is better known for *Zum ewigen Frieden* (1795) *available at:* http://www.mda.de/homes/matban/de/kant-zef.html. His metaphysics and idealism led him to be rejected because only material facts are capable of scientific proof not opinions or subjective states of mind. "Liberal" is a much abused term, particularly by "neo" "liberals". To understand the origin and true meaning of the concept of liberality (and by consequence that "neo-liberal" thought is in fact illiberal) *see:* Aristotle, *Nichomachean Ethics,* Book IV Ch. 1 *supra* note 445 *at:* http://classics.mit.edu/Aristotle/nicomachaen.4.iv.html.

[257] Karl Marx, *Kapital I*. MEW 23, 189f.309, 183, 789 (1867), *available at:* http://www.marx-forum.de/das_kapital/kapital_1/inhalt_1.html. Friedrich Engels, *Anti-Dühring,* MEW, 20, 95-99. (1887) *available at:* http://www.mlwerke.de/me/me20/me20_001.htm. V.I. Lenin, *The State and Revolution,* Collected Works, Volume 25, p. 381-492 (1918) *available at:* http://www.marxists.org/archive/lenin/works/1917/sep/staterev/. Mao Tse-tung, "On Policy (1940)," *Selected Works of Mao Tse-tung,* Foreign Languages Press, Peking 1965, Vol. II, pp. 441-49. *Available at:* http://www.marx2mao.org/Mao/OP40.html.

[258] For an exposé and critique of the conventional wisdom *see:* Scott D. Syfert, "Capitalism Or Corruption? Corporate Structure, Western Investment And Commercial Crime In The Russian Federation," 18 *N.Y.L. Sch. J. Int'l & Comp. L.* 357, 357 (1999).

[259] Shannan C. Krasnokutski, "Human Rights In Transition: The Success And Failure Of Polish And Russian Criminal Justice Reform," 33 *Case W. Res. J. Int'l L.* 13 to 33 *Case W. Res. J. Int'l L.* 13, 13 (2001). Louise Shelley, "Post-Soviet Organised Crime And The Rule Of Law," 28 *J. Marshall L. Rev.* 827 (1995) ("Organised crime in Russia today is so serious that it threatens human rights, the rule of law, democracy, and free markets").

legal equality, at least in theory, of blacks and whites. However formal equality is not the same as substantive equality. Formal improvements in post-Apartheid South Africa are belied, just as in Russia, Burma, Yugoslavia, and Nigeria, by the rise in crime which has occurred in South Africa since 1989—although perhaps a net human rights improvement can be seen in South America.[260] What conclusions can we draw from these facts?

c. Conclusions

Rights can only be understood in their economic context because rights are ultimately claims to material goods or determine procedures by which material goods are assigned. Rights can only be scientifically understood when we see them as arising out of material conditions because science requires empirical verification of propositions. The fact that the conceptualization of rights has evolved with economic progress corroborates the theory that rights can only be understood from a materialist perspective. It is possible that the resurgence of property[261] and market rights such as capital mobility[262] and the free movement of labour and goods in the post-Soviet world may be merely a temporary trend until the third world objections to capitalism reorganize.[263] Such

---

[260] Id. Louise Shelley, "Post-Soviet Organised Crime And The Rule Of Law," 28 *J. Marshall L. Rev.* 827 (1995). Christopher C. Joyner, "Enforcing Human Rights Standards In The Former Yugoslavia: The Case For An International War Crimes Tribunal," 22 *Denv. J. Int'l L. & Pol'y* 235, 251 (1994). Sakak Mahmud, "The Failed Transition to Civilian Rule in Nigeria: Implications for Democracy and Human Rights," 40 *Afr. Today* 87 (1993); Okechukwu Oko, "Subverting The Scourge Of Corruption In Nigeria: A Reform Prospectus," 34 *N.Y.U. J. Int'l L. & Pol.* 397 to 34 *N.Y.U. J. Int'l L. & Pol.* 397, 397 (2002). Adrien Katherine Wing, "The South African Transition To Democratic Rule: Lessons For International And Comparative Law," 94 *Am. Soc'y Int'l L. Proc.* 254, 259 (2000).

[261] See, e.g., *Loizidou v. Turkey* (Merits) (ECHR 40/1993/435/514) (1996).

[262] Alfred C. Aman, *supra* note *42* at 781. (Points out global capital mobility; It must be remembered that prior to 1970 international capital mobility was the exception, not the rule).

[263] Jost Delbruck argues that major changes have occurred in international relations and international law since 1989 — but that these changes actually affirm sovereignty (*supra* note *103 at* 705). However Delbruck himself acknowledges both the disintegration of states such as the U.S.S.R. into smaller states (id.) and more importantly the rise of transnational institutions of governance (id. at 706). The devolution of the sovereign power to other sovereigns cannot be seen as an affirmation of sovereignty but is evidence of its transformation. Further the transnational institutions of global governance clearly

reorganization could possibly be centered around local cultural icons such as religious fundamentalism, e.g. Islamic nationalism,[264] liberation theology[265] or some other mix of ancient and modern local resistance to a global economic order.[266] On the other hand, it is also possible that the rise of market rights since 1989 could be signalling the return to an understanding of rights in the first generational sense as mere limits on the state's power or right to constrain the market ("freedoms from") rather than positive claims to substantive resources ("rights to").[267]

As we have seen the usual tri-partite generational perspective on human rights is only partially complete. This is because that classification ignores both the economic foundation of human rights and their social expansion to cover not only white male adult citizens but also women, persons of color and even children.[268] The classical typology is incomplete but does however help us understand rights discourse although only partially. Human rights are a truly universal concept existing in different cultures and places throughout history because they are an expression of a common yet uniquely human capacity: logic.

---

affirm the fact that sovereignty has been not only transformed by devolution but also transferred by so many derogations that to speak of a rule of absolute sovereignty is meaningless and to speak of literally dozens of exceptions to a principle of qualified sovereignty is awkward. It would be better theoretically to reconceptualise sovereignty rather than to deny empirical reality in order to affirm outdated dogma. Jost Delbruck, *supra* note 91 at 705-706.

[264] For an interesting discussion of the convergence of local tribalism and globalization *see:* Benjamin R. Barber, *Jihad Vs. McWorld* (Times Books, 1995).

[265] See, e.g., Mark Engler, "Toward the 'Rights of the Poor': Human Rights in Liberation Theology,"

Journal Of Rights and Ethics, JRE 28.3:337-63 (2000).

[266] As mentioned elsewhere the world is developing institutions and processes of global governance under law. Ulrich K. Preuss *supra* note 113 at 305-306. International institutions such as the European Union and the W.T.O. and the U.N. are in fact replacing so many functions of the state that, in concert with devolution and privatization, we can meaningfully speak of a shift of state power from the nation state to regional global and local institutions of governance.

[267] Some predict that claims that Western ideals are universal will increase because of the end of the cold war. *See:* Dianne Otto *supra* note 168 at 1.

[268] T. S. Twibell, "Ethiopian Constitutional Law: The Structure Of The Ethiopian Government And The New Constitution's Ability To Overcome Ethiopia's Problems," 21 *Loy. L.A. Int'l & Comp. L.J.* 399, 399 (1999).

BOOK REVIEWS

MULTICULTURALISM AND "THE POLITICS OF RECOGNITION"
By Charles Taylor, et. al. (Edited by Amy Gutmann)
PRINCETON UNIVERSITY PRESS, 1992.

Reviewed by Charles Brian McAdams
Department of Religion, Temple University

CHERISHING CULTURES

There is much to commend Charles Taylor's essay which explores the often heated debates over multiculturalism. The book avoids polemical pitfalls and is both thoughtful and thought provoking. In terms of format, in addition to Taylor's essay, the book contains an introduction by Amy Gutmann and responses by Susan Wolf, Steven C. Rockefeller, and Michael Walzer. These comments further the conversation helpfully. Nevertheless, for the sake of space, I confine my remarks to Taylor's essay.

When applied to the debates over multiculturalism, Taylor contends that contemporary liberal democracies have two conflicting goals: treating everyone equally and recognizing the value of individuals and their collective cultures. (43) Framed as a question: should democratic institutions treat everyone and every culture the same regardless of their individual differences, or should democratic institutions embrace the differences that result from cultural diversity? Taylor uses two effective examples, Quebec's laws embracing the uniqueness of its culture contrasted with the Canadian charter's demand for equal treatment of all (52-56), and the debate over liberal arts curricula—whether they should be reformed to include more female and "non-western" voices. (65-73)

Taylor advocates for policies which embrace difference, like Quebec's laws which encourage or mandate French (so long as basic liberties are maintained), or policies which expand the canon to include more diversity. He asserts that,

> it is reasonable to suppose that cultures that have provided the horizon of meaning for large numbers of human beings, of diverse characters and temperaments, over a long period of

> time–that have, in other words, articulated their sense of the good, the holy, the admirable–are almost certain to have something that deserves our admiration and respect, even if it is accompanied by much that we have to abhor and reject. Perhaps one could put it another way: it would take a supreme arrogance to discount this possibility *a priori*. (72-3)

Denying the possibility of such contributions is "a supreme arrogance." Regardless of how praiseworthy one believes "western" culture is, certainly it does not have a monopoly on all that is good and valuable. Taylor continues that,

> what this presumption requires of us is not peremptory and inauthentic judgments of equal value, but a willingness to be open to comparative cultural study of the kind that must displace our horizons in the resulting fusions. (73)

Taylor argues against assuming that "western" society has a monopoly on excellence, but he also cautions against prematurely concluding that all cultures' contributions are equally valuable. Instead, he advocates for learning about other cultures with an openness to the transformation of even the standards by which we judge the worth of other cultures, resulting in a more "dialogical" interaction. (32)

Therefore, democratic institutions can enact policies that recognize difference. Taylor distinguishes himself from Ronald Dworkin, saying that Dworkin believes a "liberal society must remain neutral on the good life, and restrict itself to ensuring that however they see things, citizens deal fairly with each other and the state deal equally with all." (57) In contrast, Taylor argues that "liberalism can't and shouldn't claim complete neutrality." (62) In fact, he argues, even the idea of the secular, is rooted in a particular culture, as "secular" is itself an idea taken from Christianity. (62) Instead Taylor advocates for a liberalism which acknowledges that it is seeking a good, that is not just procedural, but still protects "fundamental liberties" of all people. (59) For Taylor, the recognition and preservation of cultural differences is one such good.

Throughout his essay, Taylor links multiculturalism and efforts to preserve cultures. For example, while discussing the Canadian example, he says, "what is at stake was the desire of these people for *survival*, and their consequent demand for certain forms of autonomy in their self-government, as well as the ability to adopt certain kinds of legislation deemed necessary for *survival*." (52, emphases added, see also 63, 64) He likewise sets cultural protection as a goal. (53, footnote number 29) as well as "preservation" (58) and maintenance of distinctiveness. (40) While I support the values of multiculturalism, I urge caution in the use of the language of preservation.

Consider, for instance, Taylor's second example, the western canon. I contend that a multicultural curriculum does not serve to protect or preserve culture as education creates culture. A liberal arts education does not just teach about cultures, but it also contributes to the creation and production of cultures. A curriculum designed to include previously excluded works contributes to the creation a new culture, one that, we hope, respects the value of the various cultures included in the curriculum. Therefore, using a multicultural curriculum does not actually contribute to the survival, protection or preservation of the individual cultures included in it, but, in fact, instead contributes to the *production* of a culture (or cultures) as liberal arts education always does. I suspect that most, if not all, educators hope their teaching transforms their students. This change then affects the cultures of which the students are a part. As such, a liberal arts education is about cultural production rather than preservation.

Though preservation/protection/survival may be an unfeasible goal for a multicultural curriculum, multiculturalism can, and I contend should, encourage the cherishing of the valuable contributions from the vast varieties of cultures of the world. Yet, these cultures and the cultures produced by multiculturalism will continue to change and adapt. As such I wish to suggest cherishing as a goal (instead of preserving and protecting) as it still challenges the normalization of hegemonic cultures and counters the forces of homogenization. (52)

Certainly the goal of cherishing is not absent from Taylor's essay. (40) He also speaks of "the study of the other" as transforming. (70) He rightly says "[b]ooks do more than inspire, they also unite us in a community, or communities of learning." (17) In fact, his argument presupposes that engaging the other can change cultures. But the central focus should be more fully on the goal of cherishing of cultures, vis á vis its preservation, as this goal seems more feasible and helpful.

Though I wish Taylor had set "cherishing" as the goal of multiculturalism, instead of focusing on "preserving," his essay is quite helpful. It helps to move the debate beyond polemics and it articulates a vision for democratic institutions which embraces multiculturalism. Packaging Taylor's essay with commentaries upon it further encourages a respectful thoughtful debate over multiculturalism. More than a decade after the book's publication, it continues to be a valuable contribution amidst ongoing, heated debates.

NATURAL LAW: AN INTRODUCTION AND RE-EXAMINATION
By Howard P. Kainz
Open Court Press, 2004

Reviewed by Robert L. Chapman
Department of Philosophy & Religious Studies
Pace University, New York City

As the title indicates this is not just another introduction to natural law to add to the vast collection already out there; fortunately the book undertakes, successfully, I think, a serious "re-examination" of natural law. Not that the "Introduction" should be dismissed; Kainz provides a comprehensive history of the evolution of natural law touching on the standard favorites—Plato, Aristotle, the Stoics, Aquinas, Hobbes, Locke, Grotius, Pufendorf and with qualifications, Kant. The inclusion of Francisco Suarez and Richard Cumberland as critical responses to Aquinas and Hobbes, respectively, heightens the historical drama. The 'new' natural law theory is also well represented by John Finnis and Germain Grisez, along with their more notable critics—Robert Scavone, Ralph McInerny, and Robert Lisska. But the distinguishing difference between Kainz's book and the more recent additions to the literature is his clear and highly developed exposition of problem areas, different classifications, and applications of natural law. My review, therefore, concentrates almost exclusively on what I imagine as 'Part II', which begins with chapter 5—"Conceptual Analyses of Issues in Natural – Law Theory." This is clearly not the intention of Professor Kainz. I impose this taxonomy mainly to extol a desirable quality of his text: amplified pedagogical application—it well serves student audiences from undergraduate freshmen to first-year graduate students along with those outside the academy who are so inclined.

Professor Kainz begins his examination of natural law [hereafter NL] at the beginning with an inquiry into the meaning(s) of nature, natural, and law. Kainz's critical questions: "Can natural law as a strictly philosophical theory, independent of theological commitments and the idea of a divine lawgiver, be a *law* in any meaningful way…" and a 'meaningful way' means, "...as something promulgated for the common good, and associated with commands and penalties for infractions?" (55) With recourse to Plato, Aristotle, the Stoics et al, Kainz scrutinizes the various meanings of "nature", "natural", "unnaturality", and "perversion" by parading veteran and familiar definitions/descriptions of 'nature' and 'natural' along with problems associated with each. But when discussing the NewNL—influenced as it is by scientific discoveries and technological innovations—other explanations are required to accommodate the turn away from theological and divine underpinnings. It is here that the "re-examination" begins to come together.

Following Finnis, Kainz views natural law as derived from positive law; positive law is the prime analogate for natural law. (Just as the prime analogate for causality in the physical world is particle interaction.) But, he asks, what if natural law is the prime analogate and all other notions of law are analogous to it? In other words, what if experience of our actions guided by self-preservation, a drive toward happiness, knowledge and freedom (all of which are best known to us) is the bedrock meaning of law? To emphasize the point, Kainz applies this logic to the mind – body problem. As mentioned earlier the primary analogate for causality is the physics of energy and matter in motion. Thus any attempt at a solution—aside from claiming one of the extremes: materialism or idealism—to Descartes' dilemma is futile for all the well-known reasons. But if we assume that the primary analogate of causality is our experience of mind-body interaction, and then there is no insurmountable issue. Whether we accept this 'solution' is another matter, yet Kainz legitimately concludes that NL, in the sense of imposing sanctions and punishments for infractions, is only law metaphorically like the law of gravity is a law. Infractions of natural law then would be behavior that preclude the attainment of knowledge, social participation and, ultimately, happiness.

Professor Kainz goes to considerable length in chapter six considering the notorious problems facing NL theorists (especially those of the new natural law who reject theological premises): is-ought; fact-value distinction; naturalistic fallacy, teleology, etc. This ground has been gone over and over again and it would be surprising if something 'new' were uncovered. Yet contributions can be made; Kainz's contribution consists in a highly nuanced explication of Hume's theory of human sentiments, his criticism of rational ethics and the close association of these with natural law, at one point Kainz tacitly agrees that Hume was a "closet natural lawyer."

Recognizing the potential confusion regarding the difference between is-ought and fact-value identification, Kainz clears this up nicely with a brief discussion of the difference in scope between the two; fact-value is the broader classification. Nevertheless, NL theory does not fall afoul of the distinction, since the main 'fact' in NL is that the ultimate goal for humans is happiness and that 'fact' is already value-laden. This also applies to those who would use G.E. Moore's "naturalistic fallacy" to critique NL, because one cannot legitimately ask the question 'is happiness good?' Teleology is seen by many as the canker within NL that must be exorcised. But if we regard teleology not has some cosmic capper (teleology with a capital 'T') but rather as empirical observations of tendencies and developmental stages (teleology with a lower case't'), then Kainz observes we can "bracket out" the metaphysical aspects of teleology and concentrate on the concept of "maturity" or the actual unfolding of entities, i.e., oak trees and humans, etc. Earlier, we saw the necessity for NL theorists of answering issues surrounding sanctions and punishments; any law without sanctions is like an umbrella without the connecting rods. Historically the consequences for violation of natural law were: alienation, public disgrace, inner turmoil/psychic perturbations, and divine retribution. Privileging NewNL, Kainz accepts all but divine punishment. Yet he remarks there are those that would never accept NL as *bona fide* law—all those lacking a conscience.

In chapter seven, Professor Kainz aptly combines a summary of the various types of natural law, with a skilful emphasis on NL as analogy; this is an expansion on a theme from John Finnis. The author lists the following categories of NL: natural law as *strictio sensu,* i.e., sanctioned by traditional theological premises; empirical natural law or natural law by opinion; natural law by analogy. In his delineation of natural law by analogy, however, he makes room for NL in the "strict sense" by reliance on human nature; "natural law as tendencies."

He concludes his "re-examination" by applying NL by analogy to the typical problems faced by theorists: assisted suicide, terrorism, homosexuality, contraception, stem-cell research, cohabitation, and even affirmative action.

In this lean volume Kainz has achieved a programmatic synthesis of the various natural law theories whose commonality is a desire to avoid relativism by supporting a provisional foundation based upon human tendencies. The book brings a trenchant re-examination of the current discussion of ethics in ways that can only profit students of natural law.

ANNOTATED BIBLIOGRAPHY

A Select Listing of Works Illustrative of Natural Law Themes in this Issue

Works illustrative of this issue's focus—natural law and Asian thought (but also with the inclusion of Islamic thought)—and limited to the English language are emphasized in the following:[1]

ALTEKAR, Anant Sadashiv, *Sources of Hindu Dharma, in its Socio-Religious Aspects* (Sholapur Institute Pub., 1953)
[This volume gives evidence against the common belief that an unchanging "*dharma*" has always prevailed in India and that no change could be or should be considered. The author argues that there has been a continuous adjustment of "dharma" to changing conditions. He treats *nyaya* and *mimamsa*, *Atma tusti sadacara* (good and wholesome custom) and the parisad (council of elders) as some of the sources of "dharma".] Sholapur Institute Pub.

BAKHTIAR, Laleh, *Encyclopedia of Islamic Law: A Compendium of the Major Schools* (Kazi Pub., 1996)
[The various schools of law are compared and contrasted on all issues of the *Shariah* including individual worship (purification, prescribed prayer, prescribed fasting, prescribed charity and prescribed pilgrimage), economic issues including inheritance, endowments, wills and bequests, legal disability and social issues of marriage and divorce.] Kazi Pub.

BHANDARI, D.R., "Concept of Duty: A Study in Indian and Western Philosophy," *Darshana International*, Vol. 36, no. 1/141, pp. 44-47 (January 1996)

---

[1] The abstracts are mainly taken from authors' or publishers' abstracts printed on the online version of the Philosopher's Index, ATLA Religion Database, and the Bibliography of Asian Studies, as well as www. Amazon.com.

[The notion duty is essentially implied in every ethical theory. A duty means what we ought to perform as 'moral beings'. From Plato to Kant, Moore, Bradley etc. there have been very serious discussions regarding the concept of duty. It has individual as well as social aspect. In ancient Indian philosophical, social and ethical sphere it is said that the whole universe is founded on moral law called *Rita* or *Dharma* or Duty. Human duties as laid down by the *Bhagavad Gita* are determined by a man's reaction to the outer World. A man is warned to pursue his own Dharma or Duty. Here we find a striking similarity between these ideas of the *Gita* and that of Plato's ideas regarding the concept of Duty.] Author's abstract

BILIMORIA, Purushottama, "Personal Law—Legal Origins and Constitutional Issues: Debates over Uniform Civil Codes in Modern India," *Journal of Dharma*, Vol. 22, no. 4: pp. 483-522 (October-December 1997)

[The paper analyzes the colonial administration's reaction to the diversity of customs, norms and moral practices unlike the tidier common law governing a liberal society. Failure to enforce its administrative imperatives for a decent public morality and legal system led to radical legislative and juridical control with a more uniform set of penal codes and civil practices. When persuaded not to interfere with the erstwhile jurisprudence and normative texts sanctioning local customs, a compromise exempted certain apparently private habits under personal law, communally marked for Hindus, Muslims and Christians. These pertained to inheritance, adoption, succession, property rights, marriage, worship, and so on. The hybrid moral culture survived until the Indian Constitution issued directives towards uniform civil codes. Feminists, concerned to iron out the common oppressive patriarchy across all personal laws, hesitated when the Hindu right took up the cause invoking universal human rights. The paper argues the latter stance is violative of the liberal tradition, as it occludes minority rights, difference, and cultural pluralism endemic to India. Even more urgent after the Hindu right ascends to political power.] Author's abstract

BISHOP, Donald, "What is the Good?," *Indian Philosophy and Culture*, Vol. 17, pp. 142-48 (June 1972).

[The author argues that utilitarianism is valid for evaluating things but not people; hedonism is a necessary but ultimately unsatisfactory goal of life; ethical relativism and scepticism are pragmatically and psychologically indefensible; self-benefit is an inadequate motive for doing the good and the law of *karma* is sufficient justification for returning good for evil.] Author's abstract.

BODDE, Derk, *Chinese Thought, Society, and Science* (University of Hawaii Press, 1991).

BRERETON, Joel, "Dharma in the Rgveda," *Journal of Indian Philosophy*, Vol. 32, nos. 5-6, pp. 449-89 (December 2004).

BROCKINGTON, John, "the Concept of Dharma in the Ramayana," *Journal of Indian Philosophy*, VOL. 32, nos. 5-6, pp. 655-70 (December 2004).

BRONKHORST, Johannes, "Some Uses of Dharma in Classical Indian Philosophy," *Journal of Indian Philosophy*, Vol. 32, nos. 5-6, pp. 733-50 (December 2004).

BUCHANAN, Allen and MOORE, Magaret (ed.), *States, Nations, and Borders: The Ethics of Making Boundaries* (Cambridge University Press, 2003).

[This anthology compares the views and principles of seven prominent ethical traditions on one of the most pressing issues of modern politics—the making and unmaking of state and national boundaries. The traditions represented are Judaism, Christianity, Islam, natural law, Confucianism, liberalism and international law. The contributors, each an expert in one of these traditions, show how that tradition addresses the five dominant methods of altering state and national boundaries—conquest, settlement, purchase, inheritance, and secession.] Cambridge University Press.

CARTER, John Ross, "Traditional Definitions of the Term Dhamma," *Philosophy East and West*, Vol. 26, pp. 329-38 (July 1976).

CHATTERJEE, Margaret, "The Concept of Dharma" in DOESER, M.C., and KRAAY, J.N. (eds.), *Facts and Values* (Dordrecht: Nijhoff, 1986)
["*Dharma*" (righteousness) appears as moral law, Differentiated relative to factual social stages and strata. It guides the process of detachment from facticity. More profoundly than "*moksha*" (liberation), a later concept which tends to move beyond good and evil, "*dharma*" sounds the depth of both man's situation and his aspirations and seeks to balance them.] Author's abstract.

CHENG, Chung-ying, "Legalism Versus Confucianism," *Journal of Chinese Philosophy*, Vol. 8, pp. 271-302 (September 1981).
[This article deals with comparisons and contrasts between legalism and Confucianism. It gives a thorough analysis of the notion of "*fa*" (law) in classical Chinese philosophy and how it is incorporated and used in the legalistic system. The limitations of legalism are stressed.] Author's abstract.

CHEUNG, Leo K.C., "The Way of Xunzi," *Journal of Chinese Philosophy*, Vol. 28, no. 3, pp. 301-320 (September 2001)
[This article aims at offering an acceptable and better interpretation of the theory of the way (*Dao)* in the book *Xunzi*. It argues that the *Xunzi* classifies change into the change of the human affairs and that of heaven and earth, and also into begetting and transformation. Transformation is further divided into the transformation of *yin* and *yang*, *zhi* and *luan*. The *Xunzi* then defines the way as that which is in itself constant and governs all changes, and upholds a nonreductive unification of the descriptive law of nature and the prescriptive law of politics and ethics via *Li*.] Author's abstract.

COULSON, Noel J., *A History of Islamic Law* (Edinburgh University Press, 1994).

[The classic introduction to Islamic law, tracing its development from its origins, through the medieval period, to its place in modern Islam.] Edinburgh University Press.

DARSOPRAJITNO, Ir. H. Soewarno, "Natural Law as the Basis of Ecological Tourism," in PRASETYO, Truman Simanjuntak, Bagyo and HANDINI, Retno (eds.), *Sangiran: Man, Culture and Environment in Pleistocene Times* (Yayasan Obor Indonesia 2001).

DAVIS, Donald, Jr., "Dharma in Practice: Acara and Authority in Medieval Dharmasastra," *Journal of Indian Philosophy*, Vol. 32, nos. 5-6, pp. 813-30 (December 2004).

DONALD, David, Jr., "Recovering the Indigenous Legal Traditions of India: Classical Hindu Law in Practice in Late Medieval Kerala," *Journal of Indian Philosophy*, Vol. 27, no. 3, pp. 159-213 (June 1999).

[The collection of Malayalam records entitled *Vanjeri Grandhavari*, taken from the archives of an important Namputiri Brahmin family and the temple under its leadership, provides some long-awaited information regarding a wide range of legal activities in late medieval Kerala. The organization of law and the jurisprudence represented by these records bear an unmistakable similarity to legal ideas found in *dharmasastra* texts.] Author's index.

ELAYATH, K.N. Nilakantan, "Freedom of Will and Action in Sankara's Philosophy," *Vedanta Kesari*, Vol. 62, pp. 401-406 (April 1976).

[The article deals with the problem of free will and action from the *advaitic* point of view. The *upanisads* and the *ljita* by which advaitins always swear advocate denial and affirmation of free will. Sankara explains them as pertaining to two levels of reality—the metaphysical and empirical. Empirically man is free; but it is fundamentally based on the error called *adhyasa*, a product of *avidya*. Sankara, further, shows that *avidya* and similar doctrines like the law of *karma* and *samsara* do not paralyze the phenomenal free will. But the word freedom when applied to *moksa* has entirely a different meaning.] Author's abstract

EZZATI, A., *Islam and Natural Law* (Saqi Books, 2002).
[This book introduces Islam as the religion of inclusive monotheism, supporting a holistic approach toward the entire creation, including man and humanity, and taking into consideration directly all his physical, rational, emotion, and spiritual needs.] Saqi Books.

FITZGERALD, James, "Dharma and its Translation in the Mahabharata," *Journal of Indian Philosophy*, Vol. 32, nos. 5-6, pp. 671-85 (December 2004).

FRENCH, Rebecca Redwood, *The Golden Yoke: The Legal Cosmology of Buddhist Tibet* (Cornell University Press, 1995).

GALANTER, Marc, "Hinduism, Secularism, and the Indian Judiciary," *Philosophy East and West*, Vol. 21, pp. 467-87 (October 1971).
[Analysis of judicial determination of boundaries of hinduism used to generate typology of alternative modes of secularism: separation of powers; limitation; intervention. 'law and morals' and 'church and state' deemed instances of wider class of relations between law and array of 'lesser' normative traditions. Descriptive/comparative possibilities flow from generalizing suggested typology to wider class.] Author's abstract.

GANGADHARAN, S., "Origin of the Law of Karma in the Vedas," *Arasaradi Journal of Theological Reflection*, Vol. 6, pp. 30-45 (July-December 1993).

GILLEMAN, Gérard, "Natural Law, Dharma and History of Salvation" in GISPERT-SAUCH, George (ed.), *God's Word Among Men*, pp. 335-59 (Vidajyoti Institute of Religious Studies, 1973).

GLUCKLICH, Ariel, *Religious Jurisprudence in Dharmasastra* (Macmillan Pub., 1989).

GREER, Steven and LIM, Tiong Piow, "Confucianism: Natural Law Chinese Style?" *Ratio Juris: An International Journal of Jurisprudence and Philosophy of Law*, Vol. 11, no. 1, pp. 80-89 (March 1998).
[Chinese legal philosophy is little known in the West. Yet, in spite of important differences, the same central themes can be found in both cultures, sometimes interpreted in a strikingly different manner. This article discusses the many points of resemblance and the poignant contrasts between two of the most influential streams in Chinese and European jurisprudence—Confucianism and natural law.] Author's abstract.

HADDAD, Yvonne Yazbeck, *Islamic Law and the Challenges of Modernity* (AltaMira Press, 2004).
[Since Europeans first colonized Arab lands in the 19th century, they have been pressing to have the area's indigenous laws and legal systems accord with Western models. Although most Arab states now have national codes of law that reflect Western influence, fierce internal struggles continue over how to interpret Islamic law, particularly in the areas of gender and family. From different geographical and ideological points across the contemporary Arab world, Haddad and Stowasser demonstrate the range of views on just what Islam's legal heritage in the region should be. For either law or religion classes, *Islamic Law and the Challenges of Modernity* provides the broad historical overview and particular cases needed to understand this contentious issue.] AltaMira Press.

HALLAQ, Wael B., *A History of Islamic Legal Theories: An Introduction to Sunni Usul al-Fiqh* (Cambridge University Press, 1999).

[Wael B. Hallaq is already established as one of the most eminent scholars in the field of Islamic law. In his latest book, he traces the history of Islamic legal theory from its beginnings until the modern period. The book is the first of its kind in organization, approach to the subject, and critical apparatus, and as such will be an essential tool for the understanding of Islamic legal theory in particular and Islamic law in general. Its accessibility of language and style guarantees it a readership among students and scholars, as well as anyone interested in Islam and its evolution.] Cambridge University Press.

HALLAQ, Wael B., *The Origins and Evolution of Islamic Law* (Cambridge University Press, 2004).

[Covering more than three centuries of legal history, this study presents an important account of how Islam developed its own law from ancient Near Eastern legal cultures, Arabian customary law and Quranic reform. The book explores the interplay between law and politics, demonstrating how the jurists and ruling elite led a symbiotic existence that paradoxically allowed Islamic law to become uniquely independent of the "state."] Cambridge University Press.

HANSEN, Chad D., "*Fa*: Laws or Standards" in SMART, Ninian (ed.), *East-West Encounters in Philosophy and Religion* (Long Beach: 1996).

[I argue that *fa* (standards) did not change meaning when used by so-called legalists. It never meant 'law' though law was part of its denotation. *Fa* meant measurement standards and was used in Mohist ethics as a technique for "rectifying" terms and selecting a guiding discourse (*dao*). This hypothesis makes the arguments of so-called legalists more plausible. It explains how *fa* can be a method to guard against the misuse of language, reduce punishment, and be seen to protect the people (or the ruler) from officials. Laws, by virtue of their promulgation and especially when mathematically formulated, would count as *fa* (e.g., the famous *fa* that one who presents one enemy head gains promotion of one rank). However, there is no evidence that legalists had either sentential concepts or the notion of universal sentential formulae. Han-Fei-Zi showed little comprehension of what we would call the rule of law. He wrote approvingly of arbitrary, unwarned punishment. He advocated *fa* in applying codes of punishment and reward mainly to control ministers.] Author's abstract.

HANSEN, Chad D., "*Fa* (Standards: Laws) and Meaning Changes in Chinese Philosophy," *Philosophy East and West*, Vol. 44, no. 3, pp.435-488 (July 1994).

["*Fa*" (standards) never meant law'. "*Fa*" was used in ethics as a measurement standard to a) adjudicate between different ethical conceptions ("*dao*" (ways)) and b) settle interpretative disputes arising within a guiding "*dao*". The orthodoxy accepts that "*fa*" meant standards' but that its meaning changed for one school of alleged legalistic thinkers. The meaning- change hypotheses makes the arguments and attitudes of these thinkers less coherent internally as well as with the philosophical context. We find no evidence of sentential concepts in the texts. The central thinker, Han-Fei-Zi showed little comprehension of the rule of law. He wrote approvingly of ruler's handing out arbitrary, unwarned, and draconian punishment. He advocated "*fa*" (objective standards) in interpreting codes of punishment and reward mainly to "control ministers" who, otherwise, usurp the rulers control of these "two handles." His arguments for punishment are essentially consequentialist and made only from the ruler's point of view.] Author's abstract.

HASHMI, Sohail H and LEE, Steven P (eds.), *Ethics and Weapons of Mass Destruction: Religious and Secular Perspectives* (Cambridge University Press, 2004).

[This volume offers a unique perspective on the discussion of weapons of mass destruction (WMD) by broadening the terms of the debate to include both secular and religious viewpoints not normally considered. Contributors represent the following diverse ethical traditions: Buddhism, Christianity, Confucianism, feminism. Hinduism, Islam, Judaism, liberalism, natural law, pacifism, and realism. The two introductory chapters outline the technical aspects of WMD and international agreements for controlling WMD. A concluding essay compares the different ethical traditions.] Cambridge University Press.

HILLENBRAND, Martin J., "Dharma and Natural Law: A Comparison," *Modern Schoolman: A Quarterly Journal of Philosophy*, Vol 27, nos. 19-28 (November 1949).

HORSCH, Paul, "From Creation Myth to World Law: The Early History of Dharma," *Journal of Indian Philosophy*, Vol. 32, nos. 5-6, pp. 423-48 (December 2004).

IBN IDRIS AL-SHAFI'I, Muhammad, *Al-Shafi'i's Risala: Treatise on the Foundations of Islamic Jurisprudence* (Islamic Texts Society, 1993).

[Written in the second Islamic century by al-Imam al-Shafi'i (d. 204AH/820AD), the founder of one of the four Sunni schools of law, this important work gives the fundamental principles of Islamic jurisprudence and its influence continues to the present day. During the early years of the spread of Islam, the exponents of Islamic legal doctrine were faced with the problems raised by ruling and administering a diverse and rapidly growing empire. In Medina and Kufa, as well as other cities of early Muslim rule, schools of law had to be developed, but it took the genius of Muhammad b. Idris al-Shafi'i, born in the year 150AH/767AD, to establish the principles by which the various legal doctrines could be synthesised into a coherent system. In the *Risala*, which laid down the basis for such a synthesis, al-Shafi'i established the overriding authority, next only to the *Qur'an*, of the *Sunna* or example of the Prophet Muhammad as transmitted in the traditions.] Islamic Texts Society.

ICHIMURA, Shohei, "Buddhist Dharma and Natural Law: Toward a Trans-Cultural, Universal Ethics," in FU, Charles We-Hsun and

WAWRYTKO, Sandra Ann (eds.), *Buddhist Ethics and Modern Society*, pp. 383-405 (Greenwood 1991).

JAN, Yun-hua, "Political Philosophy of the Shih Liu Ching Attributed to the Yellow Emperor Taoism," *Journal of Chinese Philosophy*, Vol. 10, pp. 205-28 (September 1983).

[Based on a recently discovered manuscript the paper discusses the goal and means in the political philosophy of Huang-lao Taoism (fl 3rd-2nd bce). The idea of cosmological root of the world, love and virtue and inaction, etc., Are congruent with the teachings of Lao Tzu; but the concepts related to the establishment of an empire, the position of ruler, the balance of virtue and punishment, necessity of law and institution and emphasis on time are new developments.] Author's abstract.

JAN, Yun-hua, "Tao, Principle, and Law: The Three Key Concepts in Yellow Emperor Taoism," *Journal of Chinese Philosophy*, Vol. 7, pp. 205-28 (September 1980).

[Based on the four newly rediscovered texts attributed to the Yellow Emperor Taoism, the author argues that the *tao*, the principle ("*li*") and the law ("*fa*") are absolute and unnamable nature. Principle is the law of nature as manifested phenomena, such as changeable seasons and time, yet the law which governs the changing does not change itself. The knowledge, and the accord and discord of this law, is the principle, which determines the prosperity and adversity of things. When this is applied to society, it is known as law. These three form the triple structure of the Taoist cosmology, which embraces man, the knowledge and the nature in one system.] Author's abstract.

KADANKAVIL, K.T., "Life Vision Behind the Law Books," *Journal of Dharma*, Vol. 3, pp. 136-47 (April-June 1978).

[The aim of the article is to fix the source of influence in *dharmasutras* and *sastras* in shaping the culture and ethical convictions of Indian society. This purpose is achieved through an analysis of the content of the law-books. The conclusion of the article is that the laws and rules of conducts have their binding force from the fact that they were based on the then existing philosophico-religious beliefs of the people. Had not the compilers of the law books based their rules of conduct on the existing beliefs of the people of their time, Their directives would not have had any influence on the people as a whole.] Author's index.

KAICKER, Sudhir, "What is a Natural Law?," *Seminar* (New Delhi), No. 434, pp. 15-17 (October 1995).

KALLA, Sarla, "The Concept of Law and its Relation to Dharma," *Journal of Indian Council of Philosophical Research*, Vol. 8, no. 2, pp. 13-20 (January-April 1991).

KETKAR, Shridhar Venkatesh, *Hindu Law: and the Methods and Principles of the Historical Study Thereof* (S.K. Lahiri, 1914).

KHIOK-KHNG, Y., "A Confucian Reading of Romans 7:14-25: Nomos (Law) and Li (Propriety)," *Jian Dao*, No. 5, pp. 127-41 (January 1996).

KING, Sallie B., "From Is to Ought: Natural Law in Buddhadasa Bhikkhu and Phra Prayudh Payutto," *Journal of Religious Ethics*, Vol. 30, no. 2, pp. 275-93 (Summer 2002).

KOLLER, John, "'Dharma': An Expression of Universal Order," *Philosophy East and West*, Vol. 22, pp. 131-44 (April 1972).

[It is argued that *'dharma'* is an effect of *'yajna'*. As such it represents the order and function of the manifested world, For *'yajna'* establishes the connection with the *'rta'* of the higher unmanifested reality from which this world has evolved. Both ordinary and extraordinary *'dharma'* refer to this connection in its normative dimensions. The law of *'karman'* guarantees the relatedness of all events in the world but does not provide for the regulation of events. The ordering or regulation of relations between events is accomplished by *'dharma'*.] Author's abstract.

LOY, David, "How to Reform a Serial Killer: The Buddhist Approach to Restorative Justice," *Bridges: An Interdisciplinary Journal of Theology, Philosophy, History, and Science*, Vol. 9, nos. 1-2, pp. 75-101 (Spring-Summer 2002).

[This article considers how Buddhist perspectives on crime and punishment support the contemporary movement toward restorative (in place of retributive) justice. It concludes with some reflections on why our present criminal justice systems serve the purposes of the state better than the needs of offenders and their victims.] Author's abstract.

MAGNO, Joseph A., "Hinduism on the Morality of Violence," *International Philosophical Quarterly*, Vol. 28, pp.79-93 (March 1988).

[Despite the *"vedas"* seemingly contradictory views on the morality of violence—termed the *""dharma"*-view" (which condones violence for a just end) and the *"ahimsa"*-view" (which condemns violence even for a just end)—it is argued that hinduism yet embraces an *ahimsic* moral ideal. This is essentially done by showing that hinduism equates the *ahimsic* ideal with the law of love, and that it enjoins fulfilling this law by following one's personal *dharmic* path (conditioned consciousness of this law). Hence, to follow one's personal *dharmic* path, even if it be not perfectly in accord with the *ahimsic* ideal, is deemed the most direct and efficacious means of realizing the *ahimsic* ideal. But this conclusion itself requires justification. This is supplied by arguing that to follow faithfully one's *"dharma"* is effectively to eat away at selfishness, the antithesis of love, and so to move ever closer to realizing the law of love and the *ahimsic* ideal.] Author's abstract.

MALKANI, G.R., "The Rationale of the Law of Karma," *Philosophical Quarterly* (India), Vol. 37, pp. 257-66.

MALKANI, G.R., "Some Criticisms of the Karmic Law by Professor Warren E. Steinkraus Answered," *Philosophical Quarterly* (India), Vol. 38, pp. 155-62.

MANICKAM, T.M., "Law and Morality in Hindu Dharma," *Journal of Dharma*, Vol. 4, pp. 388-97 (October-December 1979).

MAY, Reinhard May, *Law and Society East and West: Dharma, Li, and Nomos, Their Contribution to Thought and to Life* (Franz Steiner 1985).

MENSKI, Werner Menski, *Hindu Law: Beyond Tradition and Modernity* (Oxford 2003).

[This book examines the development of Hindu laws from ancient period to its emergence as a postmodern phenomenon.] Oxford.

MOHAPATRA, P.K., "Ethics and the World: Applied Ethics on Indian Ethical Theories," *Proceedings of the Heraclitean Society*, Vol. 19, pp. 60-67 (1998-99).

[Ethical theories have built-in applicability to practical life; but taken in their absolute, literal sense such theories seem either inapplicable or lead to morally disastrous consequences, if applied. I therefore plead for justified violations of moral principles keeping in view the spirit of the principles and demands of the situations. Indian scriptural tradition does prescribe such violations in many cases, but its general inclination for literalism makes its celebrated ethical theories inapplicable and creates serious moral crises. Theories of truth-telling, promise-keeping, *ahimsa* and *dharma* are examined as illustrations (of the limits of liberalism and merit of 'justified' contextualism).] Author's abstract.

MOL, Hans, "Religion and Law: The Issue of Sexuality," *Journal of Dharma*, Vol. 22, no. 4, pp. 470-82 (October-December 1997).

[The further back one goes in evolutionary history, the more inseparable and indistinguishable religion (a system of "is-ness" or meaning) and law (a system of "oughtness" or morality) are. Yet nowadays they are both separate and distinguishable. They relate to one another in a dialectical way: religion contributes to (or functions for) law by integrating (legitimating) the latter. Yet in doing so it also rigidifies. The moral system contributes to (or functions for) religion by concretising it. Yet in doing so it also distorts. In conclusion, sexual restraint in the religious literature is associated with the attempt to strengthen, reinforce and sacralize group or social identity at the expense of self-affirmation. Sexual intercourse sometimes symbolizes the unity of opposite centres of identity. Sexual expression in religious literature on the other hand generally relates to bolstering self-realization.] Author's abstract.

NANDA, Ved P., SINHA, S. Prakash, and SINHA, Surya Prakash (ed.), *Hindu Law and Legal Theory* (NYU Press, 1997).

NAYAK, G.C., "Indian Philosophy and its Social Concerns: With Special Reference to the Concept of Dharma," *Journal of Dharma*, Vol. 26, no. 2, pp. 252-67 (April-June 2001).

NEEDHAM, Joseph, *Science and Civilization in China* (Cambridge University Press, 1956).

NIKAM, N.A., "The Philosophic Bases of Human Rights and Social Order in Indian Social Ethics," *Revue Internationale de Philosophie*, Vol. 12, pp. 133-143 (n.d.).

OLIVELLE, Patrick, *The Law Code of Manu* (Oxford, 2004).
[*The Law Code of Manu* is the most authoritative and the best-known legal text of ancient India. Famous for fifteen centuries it still generates controversy, with Manu's verses being cited in support of the oppression of women and members of the lower castes. A seminal Hindu text, the *Law Code* is important for its classic description of so

many social institutions that have come to be identified with Indian society. It deals with the relationships between social and ethnic groups, between men and women, the organization of the state and the judicial system, reincarnation, the workings of *karma*, and all aspects of the law. Patrick Olivelle's lucid translation is the first to be based on his critically edited text, and it incorporates the most recent scholarship on ancient Indian history, law, society, and religion.] Oxford.

OLIVELLE, Patrick, "The Semantic History of Dharma in the Middle and Late Vedic Periods," *Journal of Indian Philosophy*, Vol. 32, nos. 5-6, pp. 491-511 (December 2004).

OLIVELLE, Patrick and OLIVELLE, Suman, *Manu's Code of Law: A Critical Edition and Translation of the Manava-Dharmasastra* (Oxford, 2004).

[*Manu's Code of Law* is one of the most important texts in the Sanskrit canon, indeed one of the most important surviving texts from any classical civilization. It paints an astoundingly detailed picture of ancient Indian life-covering everything from the constitution of the king's cabinet to the price of a ferry trip for a pregnant woman —and its doctrines have been central to Indian thought and practice for 2000 years. Despite its importance, however, until now no one has produced a critical edition of this text. As a result, for centuries scholars have been forced to accept clearly inferior editions of Sanskrit texts and to use those unreliable editions as the basis for constructing the history of classical India. In this volume, Patrick Olivelle has assembled the critical text of Manu, including a critical apparatus containing all the significant manuscript variants, along with a reliable and readable translation, copious explanatory notes, and a comprehensive introduction on the structure, content, and socio-political context of the treatise. The result is an outstanding scholarly achievement that will be an essential tool for any serious student of India.] Oxford.

PAL, Jagat, "Dilemma of Dharma," *Indian Philosophical Quarterly*, Vol. 27, nos. 1-2, pp. 105-20 (January-April 2000).

[According to the Indian traditional theory of *dharma* there are two different sets of duties, general and specific, which every individual of the society is supposed to do throughout in his or her whole life. But when there is conflict between these two different *dharmas* in a particular situation, the individual faces a moral dilemma in choosing one of them. In this paper an attempt has been made to show that the problem of moral dilemma of *dharma* can be solved only by appealing to the principle of overridingness of morality.] Author's abstract.

PANIKKAR, Raimundo, "The Law of Karman and the Historical Dimension of Man," *Philosophy East and West*, Vol. 22, pp. 25-43 (January 1972).

[Traditional India has not the same conception of history as modern western culture, but it would amount to an unacceptable colonialistic attitude to affirming that it has no concept of history. If history is the way a people understands its past, *karman*—which is not a mere popular belief in reincarnation—offers the right homology for history. *Karman* is the expression of the historicity of being. Its law is the law of the 'ontological' flow of temporal reality.] Author's abstract.

PANTER-BRICK, Catherine, "Working Mothers in Rural Nepal" in MAHER, Vanessa (ed.), *The Anthropology of Breast-Feeding: Natural Law or Social Construct*, pp. 133-150 (Berg 1992).

PEERENBOOM, Randall, "Confucian Jurisprudence: Beyond Natural Law," *Asian Culture Quarterly* (Taipei), Vol. 18, no. 4, pp. 12-38 (Winter 1990).

PEERENBOOM, R.P., *Law and Morality: The Silk Manuscripts of Huang-Lao* (SUNY Press, 1993).

PEERENBOOM, R.P., "Natural Law in the Huang-Lao Boshu," *Philosophy East and West*, Vol. 40, no. 3, pp. 309-29 (July 1990).

[The recent discovery of long lost manuscripts known as the Huang-Lao Boshu has made possible reassessment of classical Chinese philosophies of law. In contrast to the sage-dependent "rule of man" of Confucianism, Huang-Lao, like legalism, espouses a rule of law. However, unlike legalism's positive law, Huang-Lao advances natural law where the laws of the human social order are predicated on and implicate the Way/*dao*, construed as a predetermined cosmic order encompassing both the human and nonhuman realms.] Author's abstract.

RAMACHANDRAN, G.N., "Philosophy of Science and Religion," *Journal of Dharma*, Vol. 8, pp. 110-18 (January-March 1983)

[The concept of the Infinite or the Supreme Spirit in Hindu religious philosophy is identical with the concept of Nature and Natural Laws as the basis of all scientific enquiry. The *Isa Upanishad* says, for instance, "By the Lord enveloped must this all be.... It is within all this; and it is outside of all this"; and the *Kena Upanishad* says, "That which mind cannot conceive, but by which mind is made to think". *Advaita* demands the oneness of the power behind existence, but exhibits itself in a million ways. All these agree with the scientists' idea of nature; Natural Law is but the manifestation of the supreme guiding power over all existence.] Author's abstract.

RAY, B.G., "The Law of Karma in Jainism, Buddhism, and Sikhism," *Visva Bharati Journal of Philosophy*, Vol. 8, pp. 71-80.

REICHENBACH, Bruce R., "Karma, Causation, and Divine Intervention," *Philosophy East and West*, Vol. 39, pp. 135-49 (April 1989).

[I explore various ways in which the *karma* we create is believed to affect our environment, which in turn is instrumental in rewarding or punishing us according to our just deserts. I argue that the problems of explaining naturalistically the causal operations of the law of *karma* and of accounting for the precise moral calculation it requires point to the necessity of a theistic administrator. But this option faces a serious dilemma when attempting to specify the relation of God to the law of *karma*.] Author's abstract.

REICHENBACH, Bruce R., *The Law of Karma: A Philosophical Study* (University of Hawaii Press, 1990).

[The book examines what advocates of the law of *karma* mean by the doctrine, various ways they interpret it, and how they see it operating. The study proceeds to investigate and critically evaluate the law of *karma*'s connections to significant philosophical concepts like causation, freedom, God, persons, the moral law, liberation, and immortality. For example, it explores in depth the implications of the doctrine for whether we are free or fatalistically determined, whether human suffering can be reconciled with cosmic justice, the nature of the self, and the character of moral experience.] University of Hawaii Press.

REICHENBACH, Bruce R., "The Law of Karma and the Principle of Causation," *Philosophy East and West*, Vol. 38, pp. 399-410 (October 1988).

[If, as I argue, the law of *karma* is a special application of the causal law to moral causation, then one has to account for the differences between the two laws. One possibility is to distinguish between "*phalas*" (immediate effects actions produce in the world) and "*samskaras*" (invisible dispositions or tendencies to act or think), and to suggest that *karma* produces the latter but not the former. This subjectivist account, however, raises questions concerning the relation between a person's "*samskaras*" and the environmental conditions which cause him pleasure and pain.] Author's abstract.

REINHART, Kevin, "Islamic Law as Islamic Ethics," *Journal of Religious Ethics*, Vol. 11, pp. 186-203 (Fall 1983).

[After arguing that Islamic law is more basic to Islamic ethics than is either Islamic theology or philosophy, the author analyzes three basic terms associated with law (and therefore ethics): "*fiqh, Shar'*", And "*shari'ah*". He then sets forth the four roots ("*usul*") of legal/ethical understanding ("*fiqh*"), describes the manner in which a judgment ("*hukm*") is reached in any particular case, discusses the taxonomy of such judgments, and concludes with some comments on the relation within Islamic law and ethics of knowledge to action.] Author's abstract.

SAFI, Louay, "Islamic Law and Society," *American Journal of Islamic Social Sciences*, Vol. 7, no. 2, pp. 177-91 (September 1990).

SCHACHT, Joseph Schacht, *An Introduction to Islamic Law* (Oxford University Press/Clarendon, 1983).

[This book presents a broad account of the present knowledge of the history and outlines the system of Islamic law. Showing that Islamic law is the key to understanding the essence of one of the great world religions, this book explores how it still influences the laws of contemporary Islamic states, and is in itself a remarkable manifestation of legal thought.] Oxford University Press/Clarendon.

SHANAHAN, Timothy and WANG, Robin, *Reason and Insight: Western and Eastern Perspectives on the Pursuit of Moral Wisdom* (Wadsworth, 1996).

[*Reason and Insight: Western and Eastern Perspectives on the Pursuit of Moral Wisdom* is a multicultural ethics textbook containing significant reading selections from both Western and Eastern ethical traditions. Ethical traditions discussed include Greek Virtue Ethics, Christian Natural Law Theory, Kantian Deontological Ethics, Utilitarianism, Existentialism, Confucianism, Taoism, Hinduism, Buddhism, and Zen. The text also includes articles on contemporary moral problems written from these perspectives on: freedom and self-direction, sexual morality, suicide and euthanasia, morality within the family, and the environment. An Introduction discusses central metaethical issues (e.g., moral relativism, ethical egoism, and the relation between religion and morality).] Wadsworth.

SHARMA, Arvind Sharma, *Hinduism and Human Rights: A Conceptual Approach* (Oxford, 2004).

[The book offers to undertake a conceptual approach to the issue of Hinduism and Human Rights in a cultural ethos in which they are perceived. It offers a rich network of interrelated questions about Human Rights from variety of Hindu and non-Hindu angles.] Oxford.

SHARMA, Arvind, "Is Karma a Moral or Natural Law," *Council of Societies for the Study of Religion Bulletin*, No. 19, pp. 92, 94 (N 1990).

SHENG-YEN, "Applied Idealism: A Buddhist Perspective on the Necessity of Government," *Harvard International Review* (March 22, 1998).

SONI, Jayandra, "Jaina Dharma as the Law of Beings and Things," *Journal of Dharma*, Vol. 22, no. 4, pp. 441-59 (October-December 1997).

[In Jainism the law of beings and things is eternal, unlike in Buddhism where Buddha is credited with having set it in motion with his famous first sermon. The word "*dharma*," generally translated as "law" is then discussed, with its technical use in Jainism. The paper then concentrates on one basic Jaina philosophical text regarding the law of beings and things and the "substances" of reality as a whole. The six basic categories of Jaina ontology are described, bringing out the metaphysical basis of the Jaina emphasis of nonviolence and its intellectual application through the theory of manifoldness.] *Journal of Dharma*.

STEINKRAUS, Warren E., "Some Problems in Karma," *Philosophical Quarterly* (India), Vol. 38, pp. 145-54.

[The persistence of belief in *karma* in oriental thought is difficult for westerners to grasp because it provides a metaphysical explanation for problems like suffering, malformation or accidents instead of offering a more plausible scientific interpretation by dealing with immediate causes. It alleges that an impersonal law of reality keeps accurate accounts of minute breaches of conduct by guaranteeing explicit punishment. If persons today suffer, it is urged that that is because of former misconduct. This is a case of illogical conversion.] Author's abstract.

STENT, Gunther S., "The Dilemma of Science and Morals," *Zygon: Journal of Religion and Science*, Vol. 10, pp. 95-112 (March 1975).

[The conflicts between science and morals which still continue to arise, despite the apparent hegemony of atheistic scientism over traditional Judeo-Christianity in the 20th century, reflect a basic contradiction in the metaphysical foundation of Western lives. The achievements of 20th century science have intensified these contradictions. Modern physics has put in question the validity of its own metaphysical basis, namely the belief in natural law, and modern biology has been unable to come to terms with the Cartesian dualism of body and soul. By contrast, Chinese lives are comparatively free of these contradictions, being founded on the philosophies of Confucianism and Taoism, to which the concepts of objectively valid truth or natural law are foreign.] Author's abstract.

SWAIN, Braja Kishore, "Smarta-Varnasrama and the Law of Welfare," *Journal of Dharma*, Vol. 14, no. 3, pp. 269-76 (July-September 1989).

[Society has its four-fold eternal divisions (intellectuals = *brahman*, administrators = *ksatrya*, producers = *vaisya*, and labourers = *sudra*) according to function. These are said as *varna* and their stage of function *asrama*, where the being earns means according to his ability and utilises as per his necessity. Law thereof is framed primarily in family and for a century. This is *smartakala*. Within this, three generations continue consisting of father, son and grandson. It is suggested that abolition of divisions which is a slogan of the politicians is devoid of possibility insofar as society is concerned. This is a psychological division. Therefore, it is indispensable.] Author's abstract.

TEETER, John W. Teeter, *The Daishonin's Path: Applying Nichiren's Buddhist Principles to American Legal Education* (University of the Pacific, 1999).

TOKARCZYK, Roman, "Universal Dimensions of Natural Law," *Dialogue and Humanism: The Universalist Journal*, Vol. 4, nos. 2-3, pp. 127-37 (1994).
[The purpose of the work is to explain how the principal message of natural law would be realized by the establishment of a universal, global and ethically good social order. Natural law in many respects is essentially characterized by universalism. Among all other functions, that it has performed in human history, its influence on the formation of social order deserves special attention. Conceptions of natural law developed first in the European tradition and were transferred to the tradition of American thought. Natural law in other great traditions—Africanism, Judaism, Islam, Hinduism, Confucianism, and Buddhism—is studied from European and, above all, American points of view.] Author's abstract.

UNDERWOOD, Frederic, "Aspects of Justice in Ancient India," *Journal of Chinese Philosophy*, Vol. 5, pp. 271-85 (September 1978).

VIKOR, Knut S., *Between God and the Sultan: A History of Islamic Law* (Oxford, 2006).
[The contrast between religion and law has been continuous throughout Muslim history. Islamic law has always existed in a tension between these two forces: God, who gave the law, and the state—the sultan—representing society and implementing the law. This tension and dynamic have created a very particular history for the law—in how it was formulated and by whom, in its theoretical basis and its actual rules, and in how it was practiced in historical reality from the time of its formation until today. That is the main theme of this book. Knut S. Vikor introduces the development and practice of Islamic law to a wide readership: students, lawyers, and the growing number of those interested in Islamic civilization. He summarizes the main con-

cepts of Islamic jurisprudence; discusses debates concerning the historicity of Islamic sources of dogma and the dating of early Islamic law; describes the classic practice of the law, in the formulation and elaboration of legal rules and practice in the courts; and sets out various substantive legal rules, on such vital matters as the family and economic activity.] Oxford.

YANG, Guorong, "Mangzi and Democracy: Dual Implications," *Journal of Chinese Philosophy*, Vol. 31, no. 1, pp. 82-102 (March 2004).

[Contemporary political philosophy can draw some inspiration from Mengzi. It offers a special perspective about social institutions and the relationship between politics and morality. When Mengzi asserted the political significance of norms, rituals and laws, his doctrines do indeed appear to be open to modern democracy. Furthermore, Mengzi's view that moral exemplars can function as norms of conduct and that law alone should not be put into practice by itself, can also be drawn upon to modify the radical inclination of modern democracy when it gives first priority to formalization, procedural legitimacy, and instrumental rationality.] Author's abstract.

WEIMING, Tu, "Joining East and West: A Confucian Perspective on Human Rights," *Harvard International Review*, Vol 20, no. 3, pp. 44-49 (June 22 1998).

[Tu Weiming is Professor of Chinese History and Philosophy at Harvard University. This article is based on an expanded version of Professor Tu's "Epilogue" in *Confucianism and Human Rights*, edited by William T. de Bary and Tu Weiming (Columbia University Press, 1998). Human rights are inseparable from human responsibilities. Although in the Confucian tradition, duty-consciousness is more pronounced than rights-consciousness—to the extent that the Confucian tradition underscores self-cultivation, family cohesiveness, economic well-being, social order, political justice, and cultural flourishing—it is a valuable spring of wisdom for an understanding of human rights broadly conceived.] *Harvard International Review*.

WEISS, Bernard G., *The Spirit of Islamic Law (Spirit of the Laws)* (University of Georgia Press, 1998).

WEZLER, Albrecht, "Dharma in the Veda and the Dharmasastras," *Journal of Indian Philosophy*, Vol. 32, nos. 5-6, pp. 629-54 (December 2004).

WUJASTYK, Dominik, "Medicine and Dharma," *Journal of Indian Philosophy*,Vol. 32, nos. 5-6, pp. 831-42 (December 2004).
[The relationship between classical Indian medicine (*ayurveda*) and Hindu ethics or religious law (*dharma*) is explored through a discussion of two examples in which a tension exists between their perspectives. In one case, the medical treatment of a sick person is in conflict with his ritual treatment. In another, meat-eating is in conflict with the concepts of friendliness (*maitri*) and harmlessness (*ahimsa*), which normally imply vegetarianism. The result of the discussion is that while classical Indian medicine valorises the traditional three goals of Hindu life (love, wealth, virtue), it give primacy to the achievement of health, since health is a logical antecedent to virtue and the other life-goals.] Author's abstract.

ZUBAIDA, Sami, *Law and Power in the Islamic World* (I.B. Tauris, 2005).
[Islamic law (the *Shari'a*) and its application is a central issue in contemporary Islamic politics and culture. Starting from modern concerns, this book examines the origins and evolution of the *Shari'a* and the corpus of texts, concepts and practices in which it has been enshrined. Sami Zubaida here considers key historical episodes of political accommodations and contests between scholars and sultans. Drawing on modern examples, mainly from Egypt and Iran, Zubaida explores how the *Shari'a* has evolved and mutated to accommodate the workings of a modern state.] I.B. Tauris.

Contributors

Peter P. Cvek is an Associate Professor of Philosophy at Saint Peter's College, Jersey City, New Jersey, and is presently serving as chair of the Department of Philosophy. He received his M.A. and Ph.D. in Philosophy from the University of Kansas. He regularly teaches courses in general ethics, contemporary ethical issues, medical ethics, and an honors seminar in Asian philosophy. He has published articles in his areas of teaching and research interests, especially in the area of natural law ethics and the philosophy of John Locke.

Eric Engle holds a Dr. Iur. from Universität Bremen, an M.Sc. in computer science from the Universität Bremen, a LL.M.Eur. from the Universität Bremen, a D.E.A. from the Université de Paris II, a D.E.A. from the University of Paris X Nanterre, and a J.D. from Saint Louis University School of Law. He has published articles on law and human rights in various law journals.

Victor Forte, M.S., M.A., Ph.D. did his graduate studies in Religion at Temple University, Philadelphia, studying Japanese Buddhism, Ethics and Continental Philosophy. He received his Ph.D. in 2004, writing his dissertation on a comparison of the meaning of the ethical in Japanese Buddhism and French Phenomenology. His essay, "The Ethics of Attainment: The Meaning of the Ethical in Dogen and Derrida" will appear in Deconstruction and the Ethical in Asian Thought, published by Routledge for 2007. He is currently an Assistant Professor in the Department of Religious Studies at Albright College, Reading PA, teaching courses in Asian thought.

R. Joseph Harte currently serves on the Faculty of General Education and Interdisciplinary Studies at Kyung Hee University in South Korea. He holds a J.D. from Michigan State University, as well as a Graduate Certificate from the Center for Advanced Study of International Development at MSU where he was a FLAS Fellow in Legal Korean for 2004-2005. He has studied Korean History, Politics and

Jurisprudence at the Graduate School of International Studies at Yonsei University in Seoul and holds a Certificate in Korean Language from Seoul National University. His research interests are in the area of Comparative East Asian Jurisprudence, Legal Development and Thought.

John W.M. Krummel received his Ph.D. in philosophy from the New School for Social Research in 1999, and is now pursuing his second Ph.D. in religion at Temple University. He has published articles on both Asian and Continental philosophy in various journals and has worked on translations from German and from Japanese for publication. His scholarly interests include Contintental philosophy, phenomenology, Heidegger, Kant, Nietzsche, Buddhism, Dogen, Kukai, Kyoto school, Nishida, and Nishitani among others. He was born and raised in Japan.

A small number of back copies of VERA LEX remain at a cost of USD $10.00 a copy.* A complete back set of VERA LEX is $115.00 (see list below). Those who order will receive, without charge, all five previous *graphically reproduced* issues neatly bound: Vol. 1, No. 1 (1979) through Vol. III, No. 1 (1982). [Vol. II No. 2 was not issued.] For more information on Pace titles, please visit the website: *http://www.pace.edu/press*

1982 Vol. III,	No. 2	Reason in the Natural Law
1986 Vol. VI,	No. 1	Edmund Burke and the Natural Law: Theory and Practice
	No. 2	Is There a Natural Law in Hebrew Tradition?
1987 Vol. VII,	No. 1	Natural Law and Constitutionalism
	No. 2	Natural Law and Constitutionalism II
1988 Vol. VIII,	No. 1	Rights I
	No. 2	Rights II
1989 Vol. IX,	No. 1	(General Interest)
	No. 2	The Spanish Tradition (Index: Yves R. Simon)
1990 Vol. X,	No. 1	Thomas Aquinas
	No. 2	(General Interest)
1991 Vol. XI,	No. 1	Equity as Natural Law
	No. 2	Sacred and Secular Natural Law
1992 Vol. XII,	No. 1	Jurisprudence and the Natural Law
	No. 2	Legal Positivism, Pragmatism

1993 Vol. XIII, **Dignity as Natural Law**
Nos. 1&2 (double issue) (Rosmini, Trigeaud)

1994 Vol. XIV, **Empirical Natural Law, Human Nature, Science**
Nos. 1&2 (double issue)

1995 Vol. XV, **Autonomy, Independence, Liberty**
Nos. 1&2 (double issue) (Includes 6-year cumulative index: 1990-1995)

2000 New Series Vol I **Natural Law and Natural Environment**
Nos. 1&2 (double issue) (available direct from Pace UP)

2001 New Series Vol. II **Liberalism and Natural Law**
Nos. 1&2 (double issue) (available direct from Pace UP)

2002 New Series Vol. III **Globalism and Natural Law**
Nos. 1&2 (double issue) (available direct from Pace UP)

2003 New Series Vol. IV **Feminism and Natural Law**
Nos. 1&2 (double issue) (available direct from Pace UP)

2004 New Series Vol. V **Medieval Natural Law Theories**
Nos. 1&2 (double issue) (available direct from Pace UP)

2005 New Series Vol. VI **The Work of John Finnis**
Nos. 1&2 (double issue) (available direct from Pace UP)

*Two back issues of VERA LEX are out of print. However, the originals are available in <u>xeroxed</u> form for USD $5.00.

1983-84 Vol. IV, **Hugo Grotius** (index)
Nos. 1&2 (double issue)

1985 Vol. V No. 1 **Giambattista Vico**
(No. 2 was not issued.)

International Philosophical Quarterly

For Over 40 Years
An International Forum
For the Exchange of Philosophical Ideas
between
America and Europe
between
East and West
Sponsored by

Fordham University   **Facultés Universitaires**
New York   **Namur**

Subscriptions:

$25.00* ($22.00 APA, $20.00 student)
$42.00* (institutions)
$20.00* (S. America, Mid. East, India, Asia and
        Africa—except in Japan and S. Africa)

*All Subscriptions outside the U.S. and Canada, add $5.00 postage.

Subscriptions or inquiries should be sent to:
International Philosophical Quarterly
Fordham University

Environmental Values

EDITOR:
Alan Holland
Dept. of Philosophy, Furness Coll.,
Lancaster University, LA1 1YG, UK

ASSOCIATED EDITORS:
Michael Hammond
Lancaster University
Robin Grove-White
Lancaster University
John Proops
University of Keele

REVIEWS EDITORS:
Clive Spash
University of Cambridge
Jeremy Roxbee-Cox
Lancaster University

ENVIRONMENTAL VALUES is concerned with the basis and justification of environmental policy. It aims to bring together contributions from philosophy, law, economics and other disciplines, which relate to the present and future environment of humans and other species; and to clarify the relationship between practical policy issues and more-fundamental underlying principles or assumptions.

The White Horse Press, 10 High Street, Knapwell, Cambridge CB3 8NR, UK
ISSN: 0963-2719 Quarterly (February, May, August, November)
Vol. 9, 2000, 144 pages per issue. Includes annual index.

Institutions: (1 year) £96 ($155 US)

(Institutional Rate Includes ELECTRONIC ACCESS)

Individual (1 year) £40 ($65 US)

Student/unwaged (1year) £30 ($50 US)

Official Journal of the International Association for Environmental Philosophy

Environmental Philosophy

$40 ($25 for students) annually with membership to International Association for Environmental Philosophy

$25 individual non-membership subscription

Send payment to:
Kenneth Maly
Department of Philosophy
University of Wisconsin-LaCrosse,
LaCrosse, WI 54601

Published by the International Association for Environmental Philosophy, the University of Wisconsin-LaCrosse and the Division of the Environment, University of Toronto

www.ingramcontent.com/pod-product-compliance
Lightning Source LLC
Chambersburg PA
CBHW021831300426
44114CB00009BA/403